NUTRITION

GENERAL EDITORS

Dale C. Garell, M.D.
Medical Director, California Children Services, Department of Health
    Services, County of Los Angeles
Associate Dean for Curriculum; Clinical Professor, Department of Pediatrics &
    Family Medicine, University of Southern California School of Medicine
Former President, Society for Adolescent Medicine

Solomon H. Snyder, M.D.
Distinguished Service Professor of Neuroscience, Pharmacology, and
    Psychiatry, Johns Hopkins University School of Medicine
Former President, Society for Neuroscience
Albert Lasker Award in Medical Research, 1978

CONSULTING EDITORS

Robert W. Blum, M.D., Ph.D.
Associate Professor, School of Public Health and Department of
    Pediatrics
Director, Adolescent Health Program, University of Minnesota
Consultant, World Health Organization

Charles E. Irwin, Jr., M.D.
Associate Professor of Pediatrics; Director, Division of Adolescent
    Medicine, University of California, San Francisco

Lloyd J. Kolbe, Ph.D.
Chief, Office of School Health & Special Projects, Center for Health
    Promotion & Education, Centers for Disease Control
President, American School Health Association

Jordan J. Popkin
Director, Division of Federal Employee Occupational Health, U.S. Public
    Health Service Region I

Joseph L. Rauh, M.D.
Professor of Pediatrics and Medicine, Adolescent Medicine, Children's
    Hospital Medical Center, Cincinnati
Former President, Society for Adolescent Medicine

Marilyn Tucker, M.S., R.D.
Registered Dietitian; Nutrition Consultant, New York City;
    New Rochelle, N.Y.

THE ENCYCLOPEDIA OF
H E A L T H

THE HEALTHY BODY

Dale C. Garell, M.D. · General Editor

NUTRITION

Anne Galperin

Introduction by C. Everett Koop, M.D., Sc.D.,
former Surgeon General, U. S. Public Health Service

CHELSEA HOUSE PUBLISHERS

New York · Philadelphia

612.3
GAL

The goal of the ENCYCLOPEDIA OF HEALTH *is to provide general information in the ever-changing areas of physiology, psychology, and related medical issues. The titles in this series are not intended to take the place of the professional advice of a physician or other health care professional.*

ON THE COVER Polarized light micrograph of vitamin B_6 crystals (pyridoxine hydrochloride). Vitamin B_6 is found in cereals, liver, and yeasts.

Chelsea House Publishers
EDITOR-IN-CHIEF   Remmel Nunn
MANAGING EDITOR   Karyn Gullen Browne
COPY CHIEF   Juliann Barbato
PICTURE EDITOR   Adrian G. Allen
ART DIRECTOR   Maria Epes
DEPUTY COPY CHIEF   Mark Rifkin
ASSISTANT ART DIRECTOR   Noreen Romano
MANUFACTURING MANAGER   Gerald Levine
SYSTEMS MANAGER   Lindsey Ottman
PRODUCTION MANAGER   Joseph Romano
PRODUCTION COORDINATOR   Marie Claire Cebrián

The Encyclopedia of Health
SENIOR EDITOR   Brian Feinberg

Staff for NUTRITION
COPY EDITOR   Laurie Kahn
EDITORIAL ASSISTANT   Christopher Duffy
PICTURE RESEARCHER   Georganne Backman Garfinkel
DESIGNER   Robert Yaffe

First Printing
1   3   5   7   9   8   6   4   2

Library of Congress Cataloging-in-Publication Data

Galperin, Anne.
   I. Nutrition/by Anne Galperin.
      p.   cm.—(The Encyclopedia of health)
   Includes bibliographical references and index.
   Summary: Examines the basics of good nutrition by studying the categories of nutrients, their functions in the body, and problems of diet and nutritional deficiencies.
   ISBN 0-7910-0024-9
        0-7910-0465-1 (pbk.)
   1. Nutrition—Juvenile literature.   2. Nutrition disorders—Juvenile literature. [1.Nutrition. 2. Nutrition disorders. 3. Digestive system.] I. Title. II. Series.
90-44364
QP141.G27 1991   CIP
612.3—dc20   AC

CONTENTS

THE ENCYCLOPEDIA OF HEALTH

THE HEALTHY BODY

The Circulatory System
Dental Health
The Digestive System
The Endocrine System
Exercise
Genetics & Heredity
The Human Body: An Overview
Hygiene
The Immune System
Memory & Learning
The Musculoskeletal System
The Nervous System
Nutrition
The Reproductive System
The Respiratory System
The Senses
Sleep
Speech & Hearing
Sports Medicine
Vision
Vitamins & Minerals

THE LIFE CYCLE

Adolescence
Adulthood
Aging
Childhood
Death & Dying
The Family
Friendship & Love
Pregnancy & Birth

MEDICAL ISSUES

Careers in Health Care
Environmental Health
Folk Medicine
Health Care Delivery
Holistic Medicine
Medical Ethics
Medical Fakes & Frauds
Medical Technology
Medicine & the Law
Occupational Health
Public Health

PSYCHOLOGICAL DISORDERS AND THEIR TREATMENT

Anxiety & Phobias
Child Abuse
Compulsive Behavior
Delinquency & Criminal Behavior
Depression
Diagnosing & Treating Mental Illness
Eating Habits & Disorders
Learning Disabilities
Mental Retardation
Personality Disorders
Schizophrenia
Stress Management
Suicide

MEDICAL DISORDERS AND THEIR TREATMENT

AIDS
Allergies
Alzheimer's Disease
Arthritis
Birth Defects
Cancer
The Common Cold
Diabetes
Emergency Medicine
Gynecological Disorders
Headaches
The Hospital
Kidney Disorders
Medical Diagnosis
The Mind-Body Connection
Mononucleosis and Other Infectious Diseases
Nuclear Medicine
Organ Transplants
Pain
Physical Handicaps
Poisons & Toxins
Prescription & OTC Drugs
Sexually Transmitted Diseases
Skin Disorders
Stroke & Heart Disease
Substance Abuse
Tropical Medicine

PREVENTION AND EDUCATION: THE KEYS TO GOOD HEALTH

C. Everett Koop, M.D., Sc.D.
former Surgeon General,
U.S. Public Health Service

The issue of health education has received particular attention in recent years because of the presence of AIDS in the news. But our response to this particular tragedy points up a number of broader issues that doctors, public health officials, educators, and the public face. In particular, it points up the necessity for sound health education for citizens of all ages.

Over the past 25 years this country has been able to bring about dramatic declines in the death rates for heart disease, stroke, accidents, and for people under the age of 45, cancer. Today, Americans generally eat better and take better care of themselves than ever before. Thus, with the help of modern science and technology, they have a better chance of surviving serious—even catastrophic—illnesses. That's the good news.

But, like every phonograph record, there's a flip side, and one with special significance for young adults. According to a report issued in 1979 by Dr. Julius Richmond, my predecessor as Surgeon General, Americans aged 15 to 24 had a higher death rate in 1979 than they did 20 years earlier. The causes: violent death and injury, alcohol and drug abuse, unwanted pregnancies, and sexually transmitted diseases. Adolescents are particularly vulnerable because they are beginning to explore their own sexuality and perhaps to experiment with drugs. The need for educating young people is critical, and the price of neglect is high.

Yet even for the population as a whole, our health is still far from what it could be. Why? A 1974 Canadian government report attributed all death and disease to four broad elements: inadequacies in the health care system, behavioral factors or unhealthy life-styles, environmental hazards, and human biological factors.

To be sure, there are diseases that are still beyond the control of even our advanced medical knowledge and techniques. And despite yearnings that are as old as the human race itself, there is no "fountain of youth" to ward off aging and death. Still, there is a solution to many of the problems that undermine sound health. In a word, that solution is prevention. Prevention, which includes health promotion and education, saves lives, improves the quality of life, and in the long run, saves money.

In the United States, organized public health activities and preventive medicine have a long history. Important milestones in this country or foreign breakthroughs adopted in the United States include the improvement of sanitary procedures and the development of pasteurized milk in the late 19th century and the introduction in the mid-20th century of effective vaccines against polio, measles, German measles, mumps, and other once-rampant diseases. Internationally, organized public health efforts began on a wide-scale basis with the International Sanitary Conference of 1851, to which 12 nations sent representatives. The World Health Organization, founded in 1948, continues these efforts under the aegis of the United Nations, with particular emphasis on combating communicable diseases and the training of health care workers.

Despite these accomplishments, much remains to be done in the field of prevention. For too long, we have had a medical care system that is science- and technology-based, focused, essentially, on illness and mortality. It is now patently obvious that both the social and the economic costs of such a system are becoming insupportable.

Implementing prevention—and its corollaries, health education and promotion—is the job of several groups of people.

First, the medical and scientific professions need to continue basic scientific research, and here we are making considerable progress. But increased concern with prevention will also have a decided impact on how primary care doctors practice medicine. With a shift to health-based rather than morbidity-based medicine, the role of the "new physician" will include a healthy dose of patient education.

Second, practitioners of the social and behavioral sciences—psychologists, economists, city planners—along with lawyers, business leaders, and government officials—must solve the practical and ethical dilemmas confronting us: poverty, crime, civil rights, literacy, education, employment, housing, sanitation, environmental protection, health care delivery systems, and so forth. All of these issues affect public health.

Third is the public at large. We'll consider that very important group in a moment.

Fourth, and the linchpin in this effort, is the public health profession—doctors, epidemiologists, teachers—who must harness the professional expertise of the first two groups and the common sense and cooperation of the third, the public. They must define the problems statistically and qualitatively and then help us set priorities for finding the solutions.

To a very large extent, improving those statistics is the responsibility of every individual. So let's consider more specifically what the role of the individual should be and why health education is so important to that role. First, and most obvious, individuals can protect themselves from illness and injury and thus minimize their need for professional medical care. They can eat nutritious food; get adequate exercise; avoid tobacco, alcohol, and drugs; and take prudent steps to avoid accidents. The proverbial "apple a day keeps the doctor away" is not so far from the truth, after all.

Second, individuals should actively participate in their own medical care. They should schedule regular medical and dental checkups. Should they develop an illness or injury, they should know when to treat themselves and when to seek professional help. To gain the maximum benefit from any medical treatment that they do require, individuals must become partners in that treatment. For instance, they should understand the effects and side effects of medications. I counsel young physicians that there is no such thing as too much information when talking with patients. But the corollary is the patient must know enough about the nuts and bolts of the healing process to understand what the doctor is telling him or her. That is at least partially the patient's responsibility.

Education is equally necessary for us to understand the ethical and public policy issues in health care today. Sometimes individuals will encounter these issues in making decisions about their own treatment or that of family members. Other citizens may encounter them as jurors in medical malpractice cases. But we all become involved, indirectly, when we elect our public officials, from school board members to the president. Should surrogate parenting be legal? To what extent is drug testing desirable, legal, or necessary? Should there be public funding for family planning, hospitals, various types of medical research, and other medical care for the indigent? How should we allocate scant technological resources, such as kidney dialysis and organ transplants? What is the proper role of government in protecting the rights of patients?

What are the broad goals of public health in the United States today? In 1980, the Public Health Service issued a report aptly entitled *Promoting Health—Preventing Disease: Objectives for the Nation*. This report expressed its goals in terms of mortality and in terms of intermediate goals in education and health improvement. It identified 15 major concerns: controlling high blood pressure; improving family planning; improving pregnancy care and infant health; increasing the rate of immunization; controlling sexually transmitted diseases; controlling the presence of toxic agents and radiation in the environment; improving occupational safety and health; preventing accidents; promoting water fluoridation and dental health; controlling infectious diseases; decreasing smoking; decreasing alcohol and drug abuse; improving nutrition; promoting physical fitness and exercise; and controlling stress and violent behavior.

For healthy adolescents and young adults (ages 15 to 24), the specific goal was a 20% reduction in deaths, with a special focus on motor vehicle injuries and alcohol and drug abuse. For adults (ages 25 to 64), the aim was 25% fewer deaths, with a concentration on heart attacks, strokes, and cancers.

Smoking is perhaps the best example of how individual behavior can have a direct impact on health. Today, cigarette smoking is recognized as the single most important preventable cause of death in our society. It is responsible for more cancers and more cancer deaths than any other known agent; is a prime risk factor for heart and blood vessel disease, chronic bronchitis, and emphysema; and is a frequent cause of complications in pregnancies and of babies born prematurely, underweight, or with potentially fatal respiratory and cardiovascular problems.

Since the release of the Surgeon General's first report on smoking in 1964, the proportion of adult smokers has declined substantially, from 43% in 1965 to 30.5% in 1985. Since 1965, 37 million people have quit smoking. Although there is still much work to be done if we are to become a "smoke-free society," it is heartening to note that public health and public education efforts—such as warnings on cigarette packages and bans on broadcast advertising—have already had significant effects.

In 1835, Alexis de Tocqueville, a French visitor to America, wrote, "In America the passion for physical well-being is general." Today, as then, health and fitness are front-page items. But with the greater scientific and technological resources now available to us, we are in a far stronger position to make good health care available to everyone. And with the greater technological threats to us as we approach the 21st century, the need to do so is more urgent than ever before. Comprehensive information about basic biology, preventive medicine, medical and surgical treatments, and related ethical and public policy issues can help you arm yourself with the knowledge you need to be healthy throughout your life.

FOREWORD

Dale C. Garell, M.D.

Advances in our understanding of health and disease during the 20th century have been truly remarkable. Indeed, it could be argued that modern health care is one of the greatest accomplishments in all of human history. In the early 20th century, improvements in sanitation, water treatment, and sewage disposal reduced death rates and increased longevity. Previously untreatable illnesses can now be managed with antibiotics, immunizations, and modern surgical techniques. Discoveries in the fields of immunology, genetic diagnosis, and organ transplantation are revolutionizing the prevention and treatment of disease. Modern medicine is even making inroads against cancer and heart disease, two of the leading causes of death in the United States.

Although there is much to be proud of, medicine continues to face enormous challenges. Science has vanquished diseases such as smallpox and polio, but new killers, most notably AIDS, confront us. Moreover, we now victimize ourselves with what some have called "diseases of choice," or those brought on by drug and alcohol abuse, bad eating habits, and mismanagement of the stresses and strains of contemporary life. The very technology that is doing so much to prolong life has brought with it previously unimaginable ethical dilemmas related to issues of death and dying. The rising cost of health care is a matter of central concern to us all. And violence in the form of automobile accidents, homicide, and suicide remains the major killer of young adults.

In the past, most people were content to leave health care and medical treatment in the hands of professionals. But since the 1960s, the consumer of medical care—that is, the patient—has assumed an increasingly central role in the management of his or her own health. There has also been a new emphasis placed on prevention: People are recognizing that their own actions can help prevent many of the conditions that have caused death and disease in the past. This accounts for the growing commitment to good nutrition and regular exercise, for the increasing number of people who are choosing not to smoke, and for a new moderation in people's drinking habits.

People want to know more about themselves and their own health. They are curious about their body: its anatomy, physiology, and biochemistry. They want to keep up with rapidly evolving medical technologies and procedures. They are willing to educate themselves about common disorders and diseases so that they can be full partners in their own health care.

THE ENCYCLOPEDIA OF HEALTH is designed to provide the basic knowledge that readers will need if they are to take significant responsibility for their own health. It is also meant to serve as a frame of reference for further study and exploration. The encyclopedia is divided into five subsections: The Healthy Body; The Life Cycle; Medical Disorders & Their Treatment; Psychological Disorders & Their Treatment; and Medical Issues. For each topic covered by the encyclopedia, we present the essential facts about the relevant biology; the symptoms, diagnosis, and treatment of common diseases and disorders; and ways in which you can prevent or reduce the severity of health problems when that is possible. The encyclopedia also projects what may lie ahead in the way of future treatment or prevention strategies.

The broad range of topics and issues covered in the encyclopedia reflects that human health encompasses physical, psychological, social, environmental, and spiritual well-being. Just as the mind and the body are inextricably linked, so, too, is the individual an integral part of the wider world that comprises his or her family, society, and environment. To discuss health in its broadest aspect it is necessary to explore the many ways in which it is connected to such fields as law, social science, public policy, economics, and even religion. And so, the encyclopedia is meant to be a bridge between science, medical technology, the world at large, and you. I hope that it will inspire you to pursue in greater depth particular areas of interest and that you will take advantage of the suggestions for further reading and the lists of resources and organizations that can provide additional information.

CHAPTER 1

NUTRITION: PAST AND PRESENT

La Belle Jardinaire, *Flemish, 17th century (artist unknown)*

The ever-expanding science of nutrition explores the link between life, health, and *nutrients*—vital chemicals needed for energy, growth, development, and repair. The human body is complex and, in some ways, self-sufficient, capable of producing a variety of substances required for its function. Because essential nutrients, oxygen, and water cannot be manufactured by the body, however, they must be obtained from the outside environment. Food is the primary source of nutrients and water. A well-chosen, balanced diet leads to good health.

Prehistoric peoples were hunters and gatherers, eating a low-calorie diet that had to be consumed in large quantities in order to obtain adequate nutrition.

Lack of food or a poor diet leads to malnutrition, which impairs bodily functions and increases susceptibility to disease.

As a species, humans are *omnivorous*. This word comes from Latin: *omni*, meaning "everything"; *vorous*, meaning "to consume." The capacity to digest both animal and vegetable substances is a characteristic humans share with other animals, including rats and pigs.

EARLY NUTRITION

In prehistoric times people gathered food—mostly roots, grasses, nuts, fruits, and vegetables, which grew wild. At first, animals and fish, found dead or caught by chance, were only occasionally eaten. This diet of predominantly low calorie foods had to be consumed in enormous quantities to maintain adequate health and nutrition. Daily life for prehistoric people was a constant search for food, which, once found, was eaten on the spot. Deliberate hunting took place once the proper tools for this enterprise were invented. Human populations at this time were commonly nomadic, traveling with the seasons as their food supply increased and decreased. This life-style continued for some half-million years.

Until fire and cooking were discovered, foods were eaten raw. It is difficult to ascertain precisely when fire making began, but it is believed that people had the means to create and use fire approximately 50,000 to 25,000 years ago. Foods such as *legumes*, or beans, which must be cooked before they are edible, were not eaten until the discovery of fire. Cooking grains increased their digestibility and yielded new foods, including porridges and breads, which were a more concentrated source of calories. As a result, the need to constantly gather and eat became less urgent.

People gained increasing control over food production with the advent of farming in southwestern Asia around 7000 B.C. This also meant the end of a nomadic existence predicated on finding food. The practices of plant cultivation, irrigation, and growing and harvesting grains, as well as keeping animals for their labor and for food, became

With the advent of fire, humans were able to make porridges and breads, concentrated calorie sources that made the need to forage less urgent.

commonplace. The human diet now became more varied and included the aforementioned grains along with fruits and vegetables, nuts, and animal products.

THE MODERN DIET

In the 1990s, United States is a nation of poorly nourished people. The American diet—high in fats, refined starches, and sugar and low in fresh fruits, vegetables, and whole grains—is not based on a natural sense of proper nutrition. It is the product of economics, modern agriculture, and the food industry.

Most people in this country enjoy access to a wide variety of food. Not only do markets sell fresh fruits, vegetables, breads, meats, and dairy products, but they also stock an alarming number of highly processed items filled with fat, salt, sugar, and artificial flavors, colors, and chemicals. These processed foods often have a long shelf life, are

The modern American diet is an unhealthy mixture: high in fats, refined starches, and sugar and low in fresh fruits, vegetables, and whole grains.

easy for markets to store, and require minimal preparation time at home, but many of them are low in nutrients.

EATING WELL VERSUS EATING RIGHT

Learning to differentiate between healthy food and junk food is a big step toward good nutrition. Even when healthful foods are selected, however, the sheer quantity of available food encourages poor eating habits. Many people eat even when they are not hungry, just because they believe it is "time" for breakfast, lunch, snacks, or dinner. Others will eat even if they are full because a dish looks and smells tempting. It is also common for people to binge on food (that is, to eat without exercising any control) to alleviate feelings of boredom, anxiety, or emotional upset.

In such an atmosphere it is difficult to determine whether humans possess an instinct for eating healthfully. Expert opinion on this question is divided. If wholesome foods were the only ones available, people might instinctively be able to put together a balanced diet. A study performed in the mid-1920s by Dr. Clara M. Davis of the Pediatric Service of Mount Sinai Hospital in Cleveland, Ohio, found that a newly weaned infant was able to select a balanced, healthy diet from the foods presented to him or her.

Yet human infants also show an innate preference for sweet things. This is an adaptive trait that permitted early humans to distinguish between ripe fruit, ready for eating, and unripe fruit, which is much more difficult to digest. In a junk-food-laden environment, however, opting for processed sweets has serious nutritional consequences.

People are often taught to eat nutritiously by making a certain number of selections daily from each of several food groups—generally, dairy products, fruits and vegetables, grains, and meats. Yet this is no longer considered the only useful way to construct a balanced diet. Some experts consider the categories too simple to ensure that people eat the wide range of foods necessary for good nutrition. This system also does not accommodate itself to the way many people actually eat. For example, vegetarians routinely eliminate meat and other animal products from their diets but, with proper food choices, still enjoy good

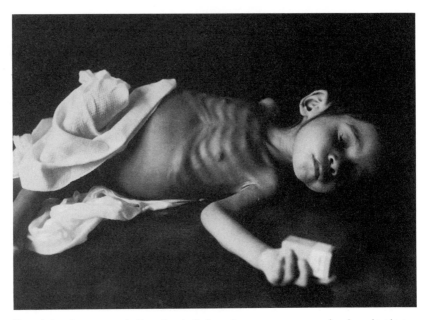

Food shortages and vitamin deficiencies are common in developing nations. Also, it is estimated that, worldwide, infant and child diarrhea kills millions each year.

health. Other people might be allergic to certain foods, such as dairy products, but can nevertheless eat other foods with comparable nutrients. *Nutritionists* (health care professionals specializing in nutrition) currently emphasize the importance of a varied diet—one with the right balance of minerals, proteins, fats, carbohydrates, and vitamins, eaten in moderation.

DIET AND HEALTH

After decades spent treating disease by means of drug therapy, nutrition is now being seen by the public and by the medical profession as an important weapon against illness. Part of this change comes from the realization that not only do individuals in the developing countries of Africa, Asia, and South America suffer from malnutrition, but people

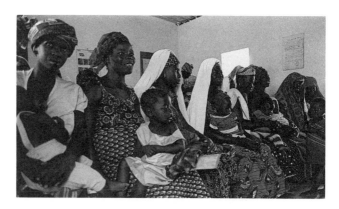

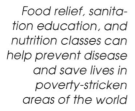

Food relief, sanitation education, and nutrition classes can help prevent disease and save lives in poverty-stricken areas of the world

in the Western world do as well. While this may sound surprising, the truth is that even an overweight person can be malnourished if he or she lacks a balanced diet.

In poor nations, the lack of clean, safe drinking and cooking water is responsible for a high incidence of recurrent diarrhea in infants and small children. It has been estimated that, worldwide, diarrhea kills millions of children each year. (To put this into perspective, one child dies of diarrhea each day in the United States.) Food shortages and vitamin deficiencies are also common in developing nations and affect people of all ages.

In addition, the most prevalent health disorders in industrialized countries—cardiovascular disease (disorders of the heart and blood vessels), obesity, diabetes mellitus (commonly referred to as diabetes), the bone disease *osteoporosis* (see Chapter 7), and cancer—are linked to unhealthy and nutritionally inadequate diets. The major health problems of developing countries in Africa, Asia, and South America are also related to malnutrition.

Public health programs throughout the world educate people about nutrition. In the United States and Europe, public awareness of nutrition is increasing, and many individuals are beginning to modify their diets by cutting back on high-fat foods such as whole-milk dairy products, eggs, and red meat, by eating more whole-grain products and fresh fruits and vegetables, and by reducing their salt intake.

In developing nations, such basics as teaching people how to prevent dehydration during bouts of sickness and to take greater care in keeping cooking and living areas clean, go hand in hand with providing vitamin supplements, food, and general education about nutrition.

DIETITIANS

Registered dietitians (R.D.s)—individuals who have studied dietetics in an accredited program and been given the appropriate fieldwork experience—are a good source of nutrition advice for people seeking to improve their diet. Qualified professionals may belong to the American Dietetic Association (ADA), the Society for Nutrition Education, the American Society of Clinical Nutrition, or the American Institute of Nutrition. The ADA can provide referral lists of qualified practitioners in an area.

CHAPTER 2

NUTRIENTS

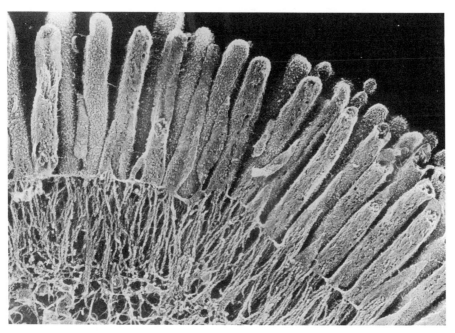

Intestinal microvilli absorb amino acids and glucose, transporting these nutrients into the bloodstream to maintain the body's energy level and keep its metabolic processes running smoothly.

The main classes of nutrients are *carbohydrates*, *fats*, *proteins*, *vitamins*, and *minerals*. The body needs them to maintain healthy cells and proper metabolism.

BASIC TYPES OF FOOD

Carbohydrates are compounds that are generally produced by plants. As their name implies, they are composed of carbon (carbo-), hydrogen (hydr-), and oxygen (-ates). The simplest carbohydrates are sugars; *complex carbohydrates* are large molecules of linked sugar groups. The body relies on the sugar *glucose*, which is broken down from carbohydrates, for its primary energy needs and brain function. Table sugar, maple syrup, corn, wheat, and rice are all examples of high-carbohydrate foods.

Fats are also carbon, hydrogen, and oxygen compounds and are made from two component molecules: *glycerol* and *fatty acid*. Coming from both animal and plant sources, fats are highly concentrated sources of energy and are required for the absorption of vitamins A, D, E, and K. Peanut oil, butter, egg yolk, and lard are some examples of fats.

Proteins are long, complex chains of *amino acids*, which are the basis of all living cells. Proteins contain carbon, hydrogen, oxygen, nitrogen, and other elements. They supply nitrogen and amino acids for every type of cell, substance, and activity in the body. Muscle, bone, cartilage, skin, blood, and tissue cells are all constructed from protein, as are *enzymes*, which promote chemical reactions in the body, and antibodies, which fight infection. Cell growth, repair, and replenishment all require protein as well. Egg whites, soybeans, fish, beef, and chicken are some high-protein foods.

Most foods, however, are combinations of nutrients, even in their natural state. For example, beef is composed of fat and protein, and milk is a combination of protein, fat, and carbohydrate. Foods such as bread or tuna salad, made from a variety of ingredients, contain many different nutrients.

ORGANIC AND INORGANIC

Vitamins are *organic* (carbon-containing) substances known as *coenzymes*, compounds that work with enzymes to help regulate chemical reactions in the body. Most vitamins are present only in food and food supplements. One vitamin the body does produce is vitamin D, which will be discussed in Chapter 6.

Minerals are *inorganic elements*—those that do not contain carbon—needed in minute quantities for the body's nutritional balance. Two examples of inorganic elements are iron and zinc.

Water is another vital substance; it makes up two-thirds of the body's weight. Water carries out a variety of functions, helping to transport nutrients and oxygen throughout the body, and aiding both digestion and the elimination of wastes from the system. People need six to eight glasses of water each day. Juices, soups, fruits, and vegetables are good sources of liquid. The same cannot be said for coffee, tea, cola drinks, and alcohol, all of which dehydrate the body. The equivalent of three or four glasses of water normally comes from the foods eaten each day.

DIGESTION

A healthy diet is not the only determinant of good nutrition. Equally important is a healthy *digestive system*—the collection of organs that together convert food into a form the body can use. Another name for the digestive system is the *alimentary canal*—the passageway that begins at the mouth and includes the *pharynx, esophagus, stomach, small* and *large intestines*, and *anus*. This is a vital mechanism because, if an individual cannot adequately process even the most nutritious foods, then he or she will not be well nourished.

Digestion prepares food to be absorbed, utilized, and stored by breaking it down into nutrient particles small enough to pass through the intestinal walls and into the bloodstream. During digestion, all nutrients are converted by stages into their simplest components: Carbohydrates are changed into glucose or other simple sugars; proteins are broken down into their constituent amino acids; and fats are converted to fatty acids.

Digestion occurs in three consecutive phases that alternate between *alkalinity* and *acidity*—first in the mouth, then in the stomach, and finally in the intestines. Acidic and alkaline are relative terms indicating the concentration of hydrogen ions (hydrogen atoms containing a

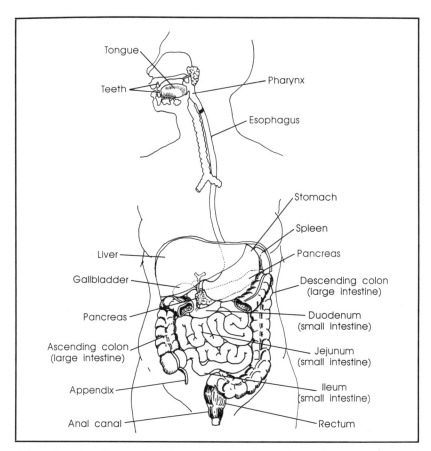

A healthy digestive system is essential for the adequate processing of food. Digestion breaks down food into nutrient particles that can be absorbed, stored, and utilized.

positive electrical charge) in a solution. The acidity or alkalinity of a solution is measured on the *pH scale*. A reading of 7 indicates that a solution is neutral, neither acidic or alkaline. A reading of less than 7 means that the solution is acidic. A reading of greater than 7 indicates that a solution is alkaline.

Stage One: The Mouth

The first stage of digestion begins in the mouth, where food is masticated, or chewed, and broken down into smaller particles. The mouth contains the tongue, the *hard* and *soft palates*, and three pairs of *salivary glands—sublingual, submaxillary,* and *parotid.* The parotid glands are the largest and sit on either side of the face, below and in front of each ear. The submaxillary glands lie below the jaw on either side of the face. The two sublingual glands lie under the tongue, one on either side.

Saliva, the fluid in the mouth, is secreted by the salivary glands when an individual sees, smells, tastes, or thinks about food. Saliva is alkaline and contains an enzyme called *ptyalin,* which helps to soften and dissolve food by breaking it down into simpler components. Saliva also lubricates the chewed food with *mucin,* which makes it easier to swallow. The muscular tube called the pharynx links the mouth to the esophagus, another muscular tube leading into the top of the stomach. Once swallowed, the now semisolid food mass is pushed through the esophagus.

Stage Two: The Stomach

The *gastric* stage of digestion begins when *peristaltic,* or muscular, movements of the esophagus propel the food mass into the stomach. The stomach is a muscular, baglike organ that flattens when empty and distends when full. *Gastric juice*—essentially hydrochloric acid (HCL)—secreted by cells in the stomach wall saturates the food mass. Gastric juice works with an enzyme called *pepsin* to break down proteins into their constituent amino acids. Another enzyme, *lipase,* begins the breakdown of fats into fatty acids.

In addition, the stomach kneads food into a thick semiliquid substance called *chyme.* Most bacteria in food is destroyed during the gastric stage. How long food remains in the stomach depends on what was eaten; for example, a meal high in protein and fat takes longer to digest than one high in carbohydrates.

Chyme passes through an opening in the stomach, the *pylorus,* which connects the stomach to the small intestine. A subset of the alimentary canal, the stomach and intestines of humans and other mammals are collectively called the *gastrointestinal tract.*

RDAs

The recommended dietary allowances (RDAs) are general guidelines to the amounts of essential nutrients needed to maintain good health in people who are not suffering from vitamin deficiencies or disease. RDAs are not minimum requirements but are set higher to take into account individual differences in needs.

RDAs are established by the Food and Nutrition Board of the National Academy of Sciences in Washington, D.C., and are continually revised to take into account new information concerning nutritional requirements. The most recent revision took place in October 1989.

The first RDA table was released in 1943, during World War II. There was increased interest in food and nutrition at the time because of national defense concerns—maintaining good health was considered one way of creating a strong nation.

The United States recommended daily allowances (U.S. RDAs) are based on but are not identical to the RDAs and are set by the Food and Drug Administration, another government agency. The U.S. RDAs are divided into four categories: from infancy to one year old; from one to four years old; from four years old through adulthood; and for pregnant and nursing women. U.S. RDAs for four years old through adulthood are used for nutritional information labeling, which is required on foods carrying nutritional claims (such as "High in vitamin C") or containing added nutrients (for example, milk fortified with vitamin D). Many food companies have voluntarily labeled products that do not fall into these two categories.

Nutrition information labels on foods must comply with a standard format that includes the following:

VITAMIN A & D
SKIM MILK
GRADE A PASTEURIZED HOMOGENIZED
NUTRITION INFORMATION PER SERVING

Serving size . . . . 1 cup
Serving per container 1
Calories 90
Proteins . . . . 8 grams*
Carbohydrates . . . . .11 grams
Fat . . . . .1 gram

PERCENTAGE OF U.S. RECOMMENDED
DAILY ALLOWANCES (U.S. RDA)

Protein 20	Niacin 0
Vitamin A 10	Calcium 30
Vitamin C 4	Iron 0
Thiamine (B1) 6	Vitamin D 25
Riboflavin (B2) 25	

Contains skim milk, Vitamin A palmitate and Vitamin D₃
*28.4 grams (g.) = 1 ounce, 8 ounces = 1 cup
454 grams (g.) = 1 pound
1 gram = 1,000 milligrams (mg.)

This mock label shows how U.S. RDAs are used to indicate the nutrition content of food.

- serving size
- number of servings in the container
- number of calories per serving
- amount of protein, carbohydrates, and fats in grams per serving
- percentage of the U.S. RDA per serving for protein, vitamins A and C, thiamine, riboflavin, niacin, calcium, and iron

Food labels often contain information about other nutrients and ingredients, such as cholesterol, sodium, and both polyunsaturated and saturated fats. Labels on vitamin and mineral supplements follow a different format and simply list their contents by percentage of the U.S. RDAs.

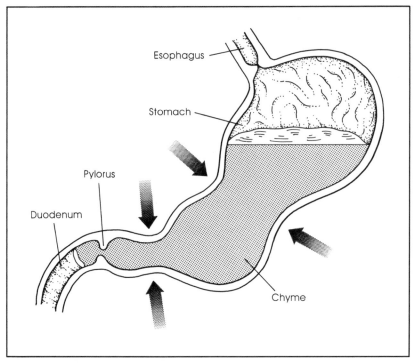

Gastric juice and enzymes in the stomach help break down food into component nutrients; the stomach also kneads digesting food into a thick semiliquid called chyme.

Stage Three: The Intestines

Most digestion and all absorption of nutrients take place in the small intestine. This 20-foot-long tube is extremely convoluted and fits neatly into the abdominal cavity. It has three distinct sections: the *duodenum*, the *jejunum*, and the *ileum*. The jejunum is the largest section of the small intestine; it also has the thickest walls, is the most richly supplied with blood vessels, and contains the most folds and bends. Intestinal secretions contain many enzymes, including those that act on sugars to convert them into usable components. These enzymes include *maltase*, which converts *maltose* into glucose; *lactase*, which breaks down *lactose* into glucose and *galactose*; and *sucrase*, which changes *sucrose* into glucose and *fructose*. A secretion from the *pancreas*, called *pancreatic amylase*, first converts starch to *dextrin* and then maltose. Another intestinal enzyme, *polypeptidase*, breaks down protein into its individual amino acids.

Many other organs work together to provide a variety of substances that help carry out this stage of digestion. These include the *liver*, *gallbladder*, pancreas, *kidneys*, and *spleen*.

The liver—located in the upper-right abdomen, close to the outside of the body—is a large organ, weighing about four pounds. The liver converts sugar to *glycogen*, which can be stored in the body until needed and then can be broken down again and used for energy. In addition, this organ manufactures *bile*, a combination of cholesterol

Bile produced in the liver, along with enzymes from the pancreas, enter the duodenum of the small intestine to aid digestion.

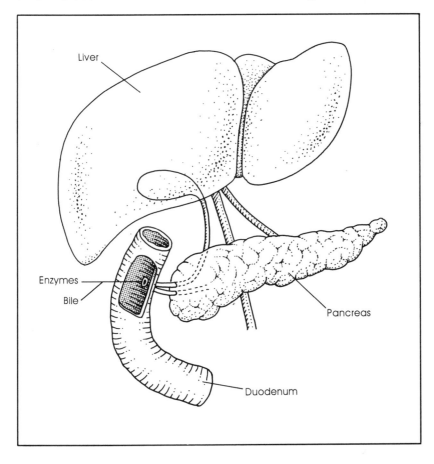

and red blood cells that is passed along to the gallbladder for storage and is used in the digestive process.

The gallbladder is a muscular, membranous sac attached at its top to the back of the liver. Four inches long and pear-shaped, the gallbladder squeezes bile into the duodenum during the digestive process.

The pancreas secretes lipase enzymes that, with the assistance of bile, break down fats into fatty acids and glycerol. Other pancreatic enzymes, called *proteases*, convert proteins into individual amino acids, just as the intestinal enzyme polypeptidase does. In addition, the pancreas produces a hormone called *insulin*, which helps the tissues take in glucose. Located at the back of the abdomen, the six-inch-long pancreas weighs less than six ounces and is shaped like a tongue. Its right side forms a broad "head" that tapers to a narrower "tail."

The two kidneys are located toward the spine at about waist level. Also weighing less than six ounces each, they remove waste and excess water from the blood, dissolving the waste in water to produce urine.

The spleen is a ductless gland about six inches long and shaped like a kidney. It lies close to the outside edge of the body above the left kidney. In addition to destroying old blood cells, storing blood, and producing white blood cells, the spleen also stores iron and copper. Generally weighing less than half a pound, the spleen's size and weight vary with an individual's age and state of health.

Nutrients reach the bloodstream in one of two ways. The wall of the small intestine is carpeted with millions of minute projections less than one-twenty-fifth of an inch long called *villi*. These in turn are covered with even tinier *microvilli*, which absorb amino acids and glucose, transporting them into the bloodstream. In addition, nutrients can also bypass the villi and diffuse directly through the intestinal wall.

Via the pouchlike *cecum*, the ileum links the small intestine to the large intestine, which is about five feet long and surrounds the top and sides of the small intestine. Undigested food goes into the *colon*, the main section of the large intestine, for temporary storage. Wastes are moved through the colon and out of the body through the rectum and anus, the bottom opening of the alimentary canal. A diet high in fiber (which is undigestible) and water produces bulky waste material that moves easily through the colon.

ENERGY AND METABOLISM

Metabolism, from the Greek word for "change," refers to all the chemical reactions that take place within the body and its billions of cells. These include the maintenance of body temperature, breathing, blood circulation, urine secretion, digestion, and formation of body cells and tissues. Every metabolic process requires fuel derived from nutrients.

Basal metabolism is the amount of energy needed to maintain basic functions when the body is at rest—but not asleep—and on an empty stomach. Basal metabolism varies from person to person, depending on weight, age, sex, and level of activity.

The Krebs Cycle

All living organisms produce their main source of energy by a process called the *Krebs cycle* (also known as the *citric acid cycle*). In a series of steps that take place within body tissues, glucose breaks down into two chemicals, *acetyl coenzyme A* (acetyl coA) and *oxaloacetic acid*. These two combine to form citric acid, which initiates the Krebs cycle. The series of reactions that follow produce energy and release carbon dioxide (which is exhaled from the lungs) and water (which is eliminat-

Dietary fiber, which can be found in raw fruits and vegetables, cannot be broken down during digestion. Fiber helps move fats out of the body, speeds up the digestive process, and helps prevent constipation.

Still Life, *Cornelis de Heem (1631-95)*

ed through urine and sweat). The cycle of reactions is sustained by the continual addition of acetyl coA.

Glucose is not the body's only source of acetyl coA; the breakdown both of fatty acids and some proteins can also be used to produce this chemical. Oxaloacetic acid, however, is derived almost exclusively from glucose. Unless oxaloacetic acid is present to combine with it, acetyl coA will produce toxic by-products in the body. This can be demonstrated in an individual who receives little or no food to eat and is therefore not being supplied with adequate glucose. His or her system is forced to get fuel from stored body fat; this in turn creates acetyl coA but does not produce oxaloacetic acid. That causes toxic by-products to be formed, including *acetone*, a poisonous, malodorous compound that can often be smelled on the breath of dieters.

When the body is forced to derive its energy solely from the breakdown of protein—during, for example, a low-carbohydrate diet or when a starving person's system has finally exhausted his or her fat stores—nitrogen is released in the process. This leads to high concentrations of ammonia in the blood. Ordinarily, the Krebs cycle would produce compounds that convert ammonia into urea, which would be harmlessly excreted in urine. In the absence of this process, however, *uremia*, the toxic buildup of ammonia, may occur, which can result in a variety of symptoms such as upset stomach, nausea, vomiting, fatigue, weakness of the heart muscle, and in the most advanced stages, stupor, seizures, or coma.

Even the Krebs cycle, however, can produce potentially harmful side effects. In addition to energy, the cycle creates unstable oxygen-containing molecules. These break down and form *free radicals* that roam through the body, oxidizing and destroying tissues and cells and creating more free radicals. This chain reaction may hasten the aging process and can perhaps cause cancer. Substances known as *antioxidants*, which include vitamins A, C, and E, protect cells from destruction by free radicals. Despite their ability to protect body cells and tissues, however, lab tests on animals have shown that high doses of these vitamins are unable to increase life span.

CHAPTER 3

PROTEINS

Fish and other protein-rich foods help maintain the body's tissues and metabolism.

The word *protein* is taken from the Greek for "in first place." Original-
ly used in 1838 by Dutch chemist Gerardus Johannes Mulder, the
word choice reflected his belief that this group of foods is essential for
human life. Mulder was right; indeed, half the human body's solid
weight is protein. Protein molecules are the structural basis for all body
tissues, including bones and teeth, hair, nails, blood vessels, muscles,
skin, and blood. Protein also helps muscles to contract and blood
vessels to expand and contract to maintain normal blood pressure, and

it is the chief material used in body-repair work, including the replacement of old tissue, the manufacture of antibodies, and the production of blood clots and scar tissue. Many hormones and all enzymes are proteins, and *hemoglobin*, a component in blood that ferries oxygen and nutrients throughout the body, is protein based as well. Almost all vital body functions rely on protein. The only substances in the body that are normally free of protein are bile, urine, and sweat.

COMPOSITION

As previously explained, protein is a molecule composed of amino acids, which are themselves organic compounds containing carbon, oxygen, hydrogen, and nitrogen. Other elements, including zinc, sulfur, iron, and potassium, may also be present. As many as 300 individual amino acid molecules link together in a long chain to form each protein. Thousands of different proteins are formed, depending on the specific sequence and combination of a given chain's amino acids.

SOURCES

The human body uses 20 common amino acids, 11 of which it is able to produce itself. The remaining nine—*histidine, valine, lysine, leucine, threonine, isoleucine, tryptophan, phenylalanine,* and *methionine*—are obtained solely from food and are known as the *essential amino acids* (meaning that it is essential that they come from dietary intake).

The proteins humans eat come both from animal and plant sources, and their nutritive value depends on the food's amino acid content and balance. Animal products and soybeans contain all the essential amino acids in approximately the correct proportions, which are one part tryptophan to two parts threonine and phenylalanine to three parts valine, lysine, isoleucine, and methionine to three and a half parts leucine.

Research shows, however, that for the most part, the plant proteins contained in legumes, nuts, seeds, vegetables, and grains and cereals

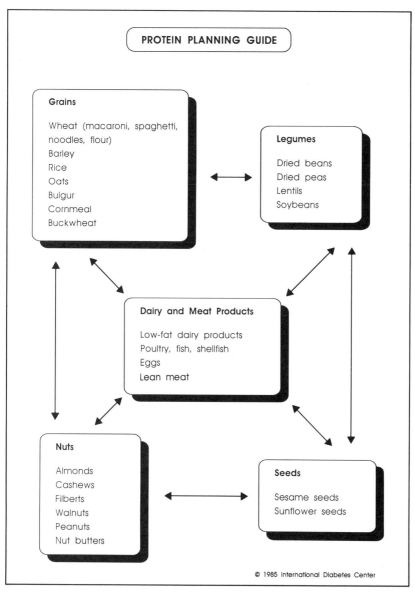

PROTEIN PLANNING GUIDE

Grains

Wheat (macaroni, spaghetti, noodles, flour)
Barley
Rice
Oats
Bulgur
Cornmeal
Buckwheat

Legumes

Dried beans
Dried peas
Lentils
Soybeans

Dairy and Meat Products

Low-fat dairy products
Poultry, fish, shellfish
Eggs
Lean meat

Nuts

Almonds
Cashews
Filberts
Walnuts
Peanuts
Nut butters

Seeds

Sesame seeds
Sunflower seeds

© 1985 International Diabetes Center

Most plant proteins are not complete (although those in soybeans are an exception). However, combining a food selection from one of the above boxes with a selection from another box, as indicated by the arrows, will create a complete protein.

are incomplete, because they lack a full array of essential amino acids in the correct balance. The body benefits less from foods that do not contain the necessary ratio of amino acids. Foods may be combined, however, so that a deficiency of an amino acid in one food is compensated for by its presence in another, creating a complete protein. Some standard combinations are legumes with grains, seeds, or nuts; and dairy products with vegetable proteins. Traditional meals, such as rice and beans, peanut butter sandwiches, macaroni and cheese, and stir-fried vegetables with tofu, create complete proteins as well. Therefore, it is possible to get all the protein the body needs strictly from plant sources.

FULFILLING THE BODY'S NEEDS

Protein is needed on a daily basis; excess cannot be stored in the body in the form of amino acids for more than a few hours. After that it is stored and used as fat. When the body does not get enough protein from the diet, it is taken from the muscles. The best way of supplying the

The majority of plant proteins are incomplete because they lack a full set of essential amino acids in the correct balance.

body with protein is to eat several small meals that include complete proteins during the day. Virtually all protein foods are *conjugated proteins*, which means that they contain amino acids as well as components of fats or carbohydrates.

Changing Needs

Protein needs change with age, pregnancy, growth, illness, level of activity, and the body's ability to produce amino acids. Protein's importance increases during pregnancy and growth, when new tissue must be formed rapidly. When people neglect adequate rest, exercise, and diet, protein needs also rise. In addition, illness, inactivity, and stress cause the muscles to lose protein and waste away, and intravenous protein is often given to people with cancer or severe wounds and burns because it helps the body repair itself and resist infection.

An individual's age and ideal weight determine the amount of protein he or she needs, although the recommended daily allowances (RDAs) for protein are on the high side. The following are the 1989 RDAs (in grams) for daily protein consumption:

birth–6 months	13 gm (grams)
7–12 months	14 gm
1–3 years	16 gm
4–6 years	24 gm
7–10 years	28 gm
11–14 years, male	45 gm
11–14 years, female	46 gm
15–18 years, male	59 gm
15–18 years, female	44 gm
19–24 years, male	58 gm
19–24 years, female	46 gm
25+ years, male	63 gm
25+ years, female	50 gm
pregnant women	60 gm
breast-feeding women, 1st 6 months	65 gm
breast-feeding women, 2nd 6 months	62 gm

(A gram equals .035 ounces.)

PROPER BALANCE

It is essential to maintain a balanced protein intake. Excess protein is bad for the body. It taxes the liver, can cause dehydration, and leeches calcium from the bones, weakening them and decreasing their mass. In addition, too much protein can place a strain on the kidneys, which have to dispose of waste products. For this reason, people with kidney disease are placed on a low-protein diet.

Americans err on the side of protein excess, generally consuming twice the protein their body requires. They also rely heavily on animal products while getting relatively little from plant sources. Although beef and other animal products do contain complete proteins, they are also very high in both fat and calories.

For meat eaters, a more desirable and healthful balance is to rely on plant sources for up to two-thirds of the daily protein requirement and to consume the remainder from animal sources. Legumes, includ-

Meat contains complete proteins but can also be high in fat and calories. Therefore, it should be eaten in moderation and balanced with other foods.

ing kidney beans, garbanzo beans, lentils, split peas, and black-eyed peas, are the best sources of plant protein. It also makes sense to use protein sources containing the lowest possible fat levels. Skinless chicken, for example, is a healthier choice than beef marbled with fat, and legumes, vegetables, and grains contain less fat and fewer calories than animal products. Nuts and seeds are good secondary sources of protein, but because they are also high in fat, they should not be eaten in large quantities.

MALNUTRITION

Although problems can result from excessive protein intake, consuming too little protein also has major repercussions. *Protein-calorie malnutrition* (PCM) is a major health hazard to children all over the world. In underdeveloped countries half the children suffer from PCM due to too little food and too little protein. PCM is also found in children from affluent homes in which the parents follow fad diets.

Pure protein deficiency, which is rare, is called *kwashiorkor*. In this, an individual is deficient in protein but not in other nutrients. A more common condition is *marasmus*, which is multiple deficiencies (including protein) caused by inadequate food intake. Protein deficiencies can develop in children who are bottle-fed with formulas that are contaminated or too diluted. The baby suffers from constant diarrhea and rapidly loses weight. Unfortunately, the problem is often incorrectly treated at home by parents who further dilute the baby's formula or substitute liquids the child cannot yet digest. Protein-deficient infants can lapse into apathy, lying still for long periods until roused, at which time they become hyperactive.

Prolonged deficiency will impair a child's growth, the production of hormones and enzymes, the body's ability to repair itself, and the actions of the immune system. In addition, *edema*, or water retention, can set in, working its way down from the top of the body. Bones and muscles waste away, a skin rash commonly appears, and hair begins to lose its color. It is difficult to determine how many deaths occur from protein deficiency because poorer nations often cannot keep adequate records. Furthermore, in the case of a multiple deficiency, it can be hard to pinpoint the cause of death.

Treatment of PCM is aimed at providing nourishment and restoring the body to health. Individuals with marasmus and kwashiorkor are usually treated for dehydration as well as for various infections. Until they can tolerate food consumed orally, feeding may take place via an intravenous needle, a *nasogastric tube* (which links the nose to the stomach), or a tube leading directly to the small intestine. Once food can be taken by mouth, liquids are generally the first step back to a normal diet. Soon cereals, easily digested fruits and vegetables, juices, meats, and eggs are provided in several small meals a day. Successful treatment depends on the victim's age and how severe the deficiency has become. Even after therapy, children who have suffered from PCM may exhibit behavioral problems as well as diminished coordination and learning capacity. Some 300 million adult survivors of PCM worldwide remain impaired in some way.

It is estimated that inadequate quantities of food have resulted in protein-calorie malnutrition among half the children in underdeveloped countries.

CHAPTER 4

CARBOHYDRATES

Rice is a valuable source of complex carbohydrates and a staple food in countries such as China, Japan, and India.

As previously discussed, carbohydrates are composed of carbon, hydrogen, and oxygen. There are two categories of carbohydrates: the simple sugars and the complex *polysaccharides*. The simplest sugars are individual molecules called *monosaccharides*. These include galactose, from milk sugar; fructose, the sugar in fruit; and glucose, a component part of table sugar. *Disaccharides* are also considered simple sugars. They are formed when two monosaccharides join together. Lactose, or milk sugar, is a combination of galactose and glucose; maltose (barley sugar) is composed of two glucose molecules; and sucrose (cane and beet sugar) is the combination of glucose and fructose.

COMPONENTS

Polysaccharides are chains of glucose linked either in a straight line or connected together into a branching structure. They are also known as complex carbohydrates. *Starch* is a polysaccharide found in plants. Each starch molecule is made up of hundreds of glucose molecules. Potatoes, grains, and beans are all high in starches.

During digestion, carbohydrates are broken down into their constituent monosaccharides so that they can be taken into the bloodstream. Eventually, all sugars are converted into glucose. Because complex carbohydrates take up to four hours to be digested and absorbed into the bloodstream, meals that include high-starch foods such as bread, potatoes, rice, and vegetables keep blood sugar levels constant and energy levels high.

FIBER

Some complex carbohydrates—such as *cellulose* and *pectin*, both of which are found in fruits and vegetables—cannot be broken down during digestion and pass through the human digestive tract intact.

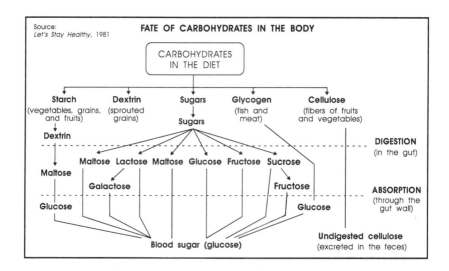

Source: *Let's Stay Healthy*, 1981

FATE OF CARBOHYDRATES IN THE BODY

CARBOHYDRATES IN THE DIET

Starch (vegetables, grains, and fruits) — Dextrin (sprouted grains) — Sugars — Glycogen (fish and meat) — Cellulose (fibers of fruits and vegetables)

Dextrin → Maltose → Glucose

Sugars

Maltose Lactose Maltose Glucose Fructose Sucrose

Galactose

Fructose

Glucose

DIGESTION (in the gut)

ABSORPTION (through the gut wall)

Blood sugar (glucose)

Undigested cellulose (excreted in the feces)

Fruit seller in La Paz, Bolivia; apples and other fruits contain fructose, a simple sugar, as well as complex carbohydrates in the form of fiber.

Indigestible carbohydrates are the components of dietary fiber. Fiber can be found in raw fruits and vegetables and in whole grains. Even though no nutritional benefits are derived from fiber itself, it is vital for several other reasons. Fiber bonds to fats such as cholesterol and moves them out of the body with the feces, thus lowering the risks of cardiovascular disease and keeping cholesterol levels in check. Fiber also helps the digestive process by hastening the passage of food through the system. In addition, it attracts water into the digestive tract to prevent constipation. High-fiber foods are also rich in nutrients and provide a feeling of fullness, which helps to control appetite. Nutritionists recommend a daily intake of 10 to 15 gm of fiber.

Fiber may also help fight cancer of the colon. Not only is fiber able to bind to other substances and carry them out of the body but it also speeds up digestion and thus limits the amount of time potentially *carcinogenic* (cancer-causing) substances remain in the body. In addition, digestive tract disorders such as *diverticulosis* and *hemorrhoids* can be controlled by a fiber-rich diet. Because fiber slows the release of glucose into the bloodstream, diabetics (who have trouble utilizing blood sugar) can benefit from a high-fiber diet as well.

Sugar and Other Sweeteners

Cookies, candy, cakes, and soft drinks are expected to contain sweetening. Many other foods, however, including spaghetti sauce, salad dressing, ketchup, and soup contain "hidden" sugar. Indeed, the majority of processed food on the market is made with added sugar. Not only does this contribute to a sweet taste, but it helps prevent spoilage, keeps food moist, makes it appear more attractive, and promotes an appealing "mouth feel."

Although sugar provides calories, it has no nutritional value, which means that an individual who eats a great deal of sugar may be satisfying his or her hunger but is failing to consume an adequate amount of nutrients. According to the American Dietetic Association, the average American goes well beyond an

In an attempt to satisfy the sweet tooth of weight-conscious consumers, food manufacturers have flooded store shelves with sugar substitutes. Aspartame, which is marketed under the name NutraSweet, is one popular example.

occasional splurge and consumes about 120 pounds of sugar each year, accounting for between 10% and 20% of his or her daily diet.

Many nutritionists believe that excessive amounts of sugar are related to tooth decay, obesity, hypoglycemia, and diabetes. But a 1986 report from the U.S. Food and Drug Administration claimed that the average American sugar intake level made no contribution to those diseases, except for tooth decay. However, a number of nutritionists consider the report misleading and inaccurate.

In an effort to lose weight by consuming less sugar, many people use low-calorie artificial sweeteners, among them *sorbitol*, *saccharin,* and *aspartame*. Sorbitol occurs naturally in fruit and is used in dietetic foods, candy, and sugarless gum. Although it has a laxative effect in amounts greater than two ounces, it is otherwise considered safe. The same cannot be said for saccharin, which has proved to cause cancer in laboratory animals. However, the FDA proposal to ban saccharin in 1977 met with loud opposition from the general public and the sweetener has remained on the market.

Aspartame (marketed under the name NutraSweet) is made from two amino acids—aspartic acid and phenylalanine. There is still some debate over the reliability of safety tests performed on this sweetener, and the long-term effects of large quantities are still unknown. Although there has been anecdotal evidence that aspartame can cause headaches and other side effects, there is no conclusive link. Individuals suffering from *phenylketonuria* should avoid the sweetener because they are unable to metabolize phenylalanine.

Water, seltzer, herbal teas, and fruit and vegetable juices are more healthful alternatives to diet soda. In addition, to reduce sugar intake and avoid highly sweetened products, consumers should read labels. Corn syrup, cornstarch, dextrose, glucose, invert sugar, maltose, fructose, and barley malt are all sugars. (Some people believe that honey, maple syrup, molasses, and brown and raw sugar are healthier than white sugar; however, there is little nutritional difference between them—they are all simple sugars and provide little benefit to the diet.) Moreover, the ingredients listed first—especially the initial five are those that occur in the largest quantities. Sweet spices and herbs such as cinnamon or nutmeg can serve as sugar substitutes, as can fresh or dried fruit for dessert or as topping on unsweetened cereal.

Vegetables are another good carbohydrate source. Eating them raw or lightly cooked also preserves their vitamin content.

Fiber should be eaten in moderation, however, because it may also remove vital nutrients from the body or interfere with their absorption. Fiber can also cause extreme discomfort if intake levels are increased too quickly.

PREPARATION AND CALORIES

At least 50% of daily calories should come from carbohydrates, with the emphasis on complex carbohydrates found in vegetables, whole grains, legumes, and fruit. No more than 10% of a person's daily calories should come from simple refined sugars.

Carbohydrates have traditionally (and incorrectly) had a reputation for being high in calories. Weight-reduction diets used to scrimp on

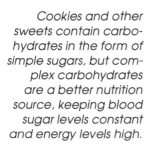

Cookies and other sweets contain carbohydrates in the form of simple sugars, but complex carbohydrates are a better nutrition source, keeping blood sugar levels constant and energy levels high.

carbohydrates and emphasize proteins instead. In reality, carbohydrates are healthy foods and particularly good for dieters because they are bulky, which makes them filling but low in calories. In many cultures, carbohydrates form the mainstay of the local diet. Rice is a staple food in many countries, including China, Japan, and India. Corn is common in both the Native American and Mexican diet, and wheat products are the backbone of the Italian diet.

However, the calorie count of carbohydrate-rich foods increases when they are prepared with excess sugar and fat (e.g., when a baked potato is slathered with butter and sour cream). Whole-wheat spaghetti with marinara sauce, on the other hand, contains less fat and fewer calories than steak, and fruit is a good way to satisfy a sweet tooth.

SOURCES

The best way to eat carbohydrates, therefore, is in the form of fresh whole fruits and vegetables and whole grains, including brown rice, whole-wheat pastas and flours, whole grains, and whole-grain breads. In addition, eating vegetables raw or lightly cooked is the optimum way to preserve their vitamin content. Frozen produce ranks second in terms of nutrients. Canned vegetables are the least nutritious and often contain added sweeteners and chemicals. Fresh juices are high in vitamins, but much of the fiber is lost in the manufacturing process.

In fact, the methods used to process many carbohydrate-rich foods commonly strip away nutrients and fiber. Much of the wheat flour in this country is refined and processed to remove at least some of the fiber-filled bran, or outside layers, as well as the *germ* (a section of the inside of the grain). Though the germ is filled with oils that eventually turn flour rancid, it is also rich in fiber and B vitamins. The grain left behind after processing still contains starch and protein but few other nutrients. In addition, flour is commonly bleached, which removes even more food value. The usual postprocessing "enrichment" returns only some of the vitamins and nutrients, and none of the fiber. Adding wheat germ to pancake, cake, or cookie batter—or anything else prepared from refined flour—will boost its nutritional value.

Corn is a complex carbohydrate source, common to both Native American and Mexican diets.

CHAPTER 5

FATS

*All animal products contain fat, a
valuable but overly abundant part
of the American diet.*

A lthough they are often maligned by a society in search of the
"perfect" figure, fats are essential for a healthy body. Fats are
organic substances that contain carbon, hydrogen, and oxygen and are
insoluble in water. As nutrients they provide nine calories per gram—
more energy than a gram of carbohydrate or protein can provide. All
animal products, including beef, pork, fish, shellfish, chicken, dairy
products, and eggs, contain fats, as do many plant products, including
nuts, grains, legumes, coconut, and avocado.

BENEFITS

Fats add taste and odor to foods, enhancing their appeal. They are digested slowly and provide a long-lasting feeling of fullness and satiety. During digestion, fats are broken down into fatty acids, and these combine with proteins, enabling the fatty acids to travel in the bloodstream and be used by the body. These combined molecules are called *lipoproteins*. (*Lipid* is another word for fat.)

In addition to supplying the body with energy, fats are important for several other reasons. They prevent skin and hair from becoming excessively dry and are a component of *myelin*, which coats and insulates nerve cells. Fats also help maintain cell tissues and membranes. In addition, fats aid digestion and absorption of fat-soluble vitamins (A, D, E, and K), fatty acids, and calcium. Hormonelike substances called *prostaglandins*—which regulate many bodily functions, including muscle contractions—are produced using fats, as are hormones and other substances.

MODERATION IS ESSENTIAL

Like any other food, however, fat must be consumed in moderation. Body fat builds up when an individual eats more calories daily than his or her body can use. Some body fat is vital, because it supports and cushions organs against injury and insulates the body against heat loss in colder weather. It also provides a store of energy from which the body can draw. Both dietary and body fats are vital in maintaining a woman's hormonal balance and regular menstrual cycle. Women who are underweight and have too little body fat can suffer from a condition called *amenorrhea*, in which menstruation ceases.

The problem is that the typical American diet contains too much fat, and a high-fat diet can lead to obesity. In addition, fat clogs the arteries and may reduce blood flow to the heart or brain, increasing the danger of heart attack or stroke. Too much fat has also been linked to colon cancer, possibly due to a breakdown of excessive dietary fats during digestion that releases carcinogens or upsets the balance of bacteria in the large intestine, making it more cancer prone. A high-fat diet may also be responsible for upsetting the hormone balance in women's bodies, leading to cancer of the breast and other reproductive organs.

CHOLESTEROL

One fatty substance, cholesterol, has received a good deal of attention recently. Labels on packaged foods often assert that they are naturally low in or contain no cholesterol, and many people are on diets to reduce their cholesterol level. The rationale behind such measures can be traced to the late 19th century, when studies first linked high levels of cholesterol in the diet and blood to an increased risk of cardiovascular disease. In 1984, the results of a 10-year study, the Lipid Reseach Clinics Coronary Primary Prevention Trials, conducted by the National Institutes of Health, indicated that lowering cholesterol levels with drugs and a low-fat diet reduces the chance of suffering a heart attack or heart disease.

Saturated and Unsaturated

Fat from food is also produced from several different forms of fatty acids—*saturated*, *polyunsaturated*, and *monounsaturated*. The word

Unsaturated fats are liquid at room temperature. All natural fats, however, are actually a mixture of both saturated and unsaturated varieties.

saturated reflects the amount of hydrogen attached to the carbon atoms in the fat. When a given fat holds all the hydrogen atoms it can, it is called a saturated fat. If a fat has space for two more hydrogen atoms, it is monounsaturated. Polyunsaturated fats are fats that have room for more than two hydrogen atoms.

TYPE OF FAT AND NUMBER OF CALORIES IN FATS AND OILS			
	Percent Poly-unsaturated Fat	Percent Saturated Fat	Percent Mono-unsaturated Fat	Calories per Tbsp.
FATS AND OILS				
Safflower oil	75%	11%	14%	125
Sunflower oil	61%	11%	28%	125
Soybean oil	61%	14%	25%	125
Corn oil	57%	14%	29%	125
Cottonseed oil	46%	29%	25%	125
Olive oil	28%	21%	51%	125
Peanut oil	14%	14%	72%	125
Palm oil	2%	81%	17%	125
Coconut oil	2%	86%	12%	125
TUB MARGARINES				
Liquid safflower oil	63%	14%	23%	100
Liquid corn oil	49%	18%	33%	100
STICK MARGARINES				
Liquid corn oil	38%	19%	43%	100
Partially hydrogenated	19%	23%	58%	100
Imitation (diet) margarine	50%	20%	30%	50
MAYONNAISE	60%	20%	20%	100
SHORTENING	25%	25%	50%	100
LARD	8%	42%	50%	115
CHICKEN FAT	26%	29%	45%	125
BEEF FAT	4%	48%	48%	125
BUTTER	trace	60%	40%	100

One cause for concern these days is evidence that has shown that eating saturated fats can actually raise cholesterol levels in the blood. Mono- and polyunsaturated fats, on the other hand, have been found to lower blood cholesterol levels. Why this occurs is still not precisely understood.

Many foods from animal sources (such as lard and chicken fat) are high in saturated fats, which are generally solid at room temperature. Plants are normally higher in unsaturated fats than in the saturated kind. These fats are liquid at room temperature and referred to as *oils*. (Coconut and palm oil are exceptions to the rule; these are saturated fats derived from plants, but they are still liquid at room temperature.) However, unsaturated fats are sometimes *hydrogenated*—meaning that hydrogen has been added—to keep them solid at room temperature and to prevent them from separating from other ingredients in processed foods.

Fish oils and most vegetable oils are polyunsaturates; these are liquid at room temperature. Corn, walnut, and soybean oils are all polyunsaturated. Monounsaturates include olive, peanut, and canola oils. However, all natural fats are actually a mixture of saturates and unsaturates. For example, only 75% of safflower oil is actually polyunsaturated.

Essential fatty acids, like essential amino acids, are those that the body needs but cannot manufacture itself. *Linoleic acid* is one example. Found in most vegetable oils, linoleic acid is vital for growth, healthy skin, and production of prostaglandins. This fatty acid also helps prevent tiny blood cells called platelets from clotting and blocking off blood vessels.

LDL and HDL

Low-density lipoprotein, or LDL, is a protein in the blood that ferries cholesterol from the liver to the tissues. High LDL levels increase the risk of clogged arteries and cardiovascular disease. On the other hand, *high-density lipoprotein*, or HDL, actually fights the formation of fat in the arteries and transports cholesterol through the blood and back to

Calories

There are two types of calories. One of these represents the amount of heat needed to raise the temperature of one gram of water by one degree centigrade; this is the *gram calorie*, or small calorie, and it is abbreviated *cal*. The second type of calorie is the amount of heat needed to raise the temperature of one kilogram of water by one degree centigrade; this is the *kilogram calorie*, or large calorie, and it is abbreviated *Cal*. The large calorie is the unit used to express the amount of heat or energy a food is capable of producing in the body; whenever the word *calorie* is used in terms of nutrition, it is understood to be the large calorie.

Carbohydrates and proteins each provide four calories per gram consumed, but fats yield nine calories per gram. Alcohol contains seven calories per gram.

Daily calorie needs start with the number of calories required to maintain an individual's *basal metabolic rate* (BMR), or a person's rate of metabolism when his or her body is at rest. The higher the BMR, the more calories are needed to preserve it. This metabolic rate depends on many factors including:

- Air temperature—a cooler environment requires a higher BMR to maintain a body temperature of 98.6.
- The number of hours per day an individual sleeps— BMR drops during sleep.
- Age—older people have lower BMRs.
- Weight—a higher BMR is required to maintain excess weight.
- Percentage of body fat—an individual with a lot of lean muscle tissue uses more calories than if he or she carried the same weight in fat.
- Gender—men average a somewhat higher BMR than women.

The number of calories per day needed to maintain a man's BMR can be roughly calculated by multiplying his weight in pounds by 12; the same figure for a woman can be estimated by multiplying weight in pounds by 11. The number of calories should also be reduced by about 2% for every 10th year of a person's life past age 20.

Aside from his or her BMR, other factors also determine the number of calories required to meet a person's needs. A sedentary individual, for example, tends to require fewer calories than someone of the same size who is very active, and a growing adolescent often needs more calories than an adult.

People often begin to "count calories" when they are trying to lose weight. One pound of fat is equivalent to 3,500 calories. To lose 1 pound, an individual has to, over a period of time, eat 3,500 fewer calories than he or she normally consumes, or raise his or her exercise level in order to work off the extra calories. Combining both strategies, however—eating less and exercising more—is the healthiest, most effective way to lose weight.

In general, a very sedentary person needs 12 calories per pound to maintain his or her weight; light activity requires 15 calories per pound; moderate activity, 20 calories per pound; and heavy activity, 25 calories per pound. Pregnancy and nursing require an additional 500 calories per day.

It also helps to know that, aside from the number of calories eaten, the source of those calories may also contribute to the amount of weight a person gains. Research indicates that calories derived from fat in food turn to fat in the body more readily than do calories from proteins and carbohydrates. It happens apparently because the body needs less energy to turn dietary fat into body fat than it does to convert proteins and carbohydrates into stored fat.

Dieters should also keep in mind that it may be unwise to make a sudden drastic reduction in their calorie intake. This can result in a slowed metabolic rate and cause the body to start retaining water. According to *The Tufts University Guide to Total Nutrition,* the wisest dieting strategy may be to cut daily calorie consumption by 30%.

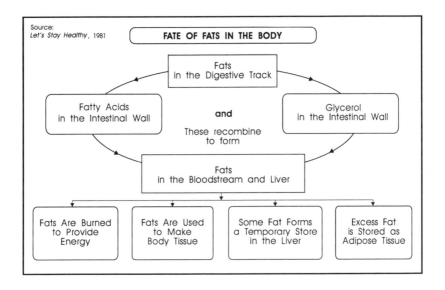

Source: *Let's Stay Healthy*, 1981

FATE OF FATS IN THE BODY

Fats in the Digestive Track

Fatty Acids in the Intestinal Wall

and

These recombine to form

Glycerol in the Intestinal Wall

Fats in the Bloodstream and Liver

Fats Are Burned to Provide Energy

Fats Are Used to Make Body Tissue

Some Fat Forms a Temporary Store in the Liver

Excess Fat is Stored as Adipose Tissue

the liver, where it can be broken down and eliminated through the intestines.

Despite the dangers of too much cholesterol, however, the human body requires a certain amount for the production of hormones and tissues. Yet the necessary quantity is already produced naturally by the body. This is called *endogenous cholesterol*. On the other hand, foods made from animals contain *exogenous cholesterol*. For many people, as cholesterol levels in their diet rise, their body responds by manufacturing less of its own cholesterol, although even for these individuals a high-cholesterol diet is considered unhealthy. For about one-third of the American population, however, the body does not compensate at all. Among these individuals, even relatively low amounts of dietary cholesterol are an excess that clogs the arterial walls, increasing their risk of *atherosclerosis* (in which the walls of the arteries become thicker and less elastic) and heart disease. Too much dietary fat may also raise blood cholesterol levels. Cholesterol levels are measured by taking a blood sample and should be decreased if there is a ratio of blood cholesterol to HDL of 4.5 to 1 or greater. Cholesterol-lowering medication is recommended only when dietary measures have failed.

Meat, eggs, and dairy products are all thought to raise cholesterol levels in the blood, which is in turn believed to contribute to cardiovascular disease.

TRIMMING THE FAT

Much is still unknown about the complex connection between dietary fats and heart disease. Because more than 500,000 people in the United States die of cardiovascular diseases each year, however, the National Heart, Lung, and Blood Institute and the American Heart Association strongly advise all Americans to reduce the amount of fat in their diet. Nutrition experts recommend that people get no more than 30% of their daily calories from fat. Yet even this may be too much. Preliminary results from a study (headed by Dr. T. Colin Campbell of Cornell University) of 6,500 individuals in China indicate that to significantly reduce the risk of heart disease and cancer, fat consumption must drop to less than 20% of daily calories. In addition, some experts believe that from the age of 2 years onward, cholesterol levels should be monitored and that no more than 250 to 300 mg of cholesterol should be consumed daily. The following suggestions will help to lower fat intake:

- Limit servings of animal protein to three ounces, because protein foods are high in fats.

- Eat poultry without skin.
- Choose lean cuts of meat and restrict intake to no more than three times each week.
- Consume pork, luncheon meats, organ meats, and duck only on rare occasions; they are all high in fat.
- Most seafood and fresh fish are a safe bet (except for shrimp, which contains as much cholesterol as beef). When eating canned fish, choose water-packed varieties instead of those packed in oil.
- Trim chicken and meat of visible fat before cooking and cook without adding extra fats (e.g., in the form of butter or cooking oil).
- Choose low-fat dairy products and limit intake of hard and processed cheeses that are not low in fat. The softer the margarine, the less saturated (and therefore the healthier) it is.
- Eat no more than three egg yolks each week.
- Consume more whole-grain cereals, pastas, and breads.

Oat bran has been a source of controversy among nutrition experts, due to conflicting studies concerning its ability to lower cholesterol. In 1986, researchers began suggesting that adding oat bran to one's diet may reduce high levels of blood cholesterol, and consumers have spent many millions of dollars on products containing oat bran. However, a 1990 report in the *New England Journal of Medicine* suggested that oat bran has no real effect on cholesterol levels. Yet many experts are still not convinced that this study presented conclusive results and believe that the question regarding oat bran's effectiveness is still unanswered.

In an attempt to attract health-conscious consumers, manufacturers are promoting snack products, such as these tortilla chips, containing reduced amounts of saturated fat.

CHAPTER 6

VITAMINS AND MINERALS

Microscopic view of the crystalline structure of vitamin C

Vitamins are organic substances that are essential in helping to regulate metabolic processes in the body. Most vitamins are found in food, although some—such as vitamin D—are also manufactured by the body. In some instances, however, an individual may not ingest sufficient amounts of a given vitamin, and if the deficiency is severe enough, specific symptoms can develop.

Certain groups of people are particularly vulnerable to vitamin deficiencies. Active alcoholics, for example, tend to have poor diets, and alcohol can cause increased loss of nutrients through diarrhea or prevent the body from absorbing nutrients adequately. (In the past, birth control pills also produced side effects that could lead to vitamin deficiency, although the problem has been alleviated in today's oral contraceptives.) Deficiencies can be treated with vitamin supplements or by adding vitamin-rich foods to the diet.

WATER-SOLUBLE VITAMINS

As their name suggests, *water-soluble vitamins* dissolve in water. Vitamins in this group are not easily stored in the body, and to avoid deficiencies it is important to eat foods that contain B and C vitamins each day. Biotin and pantothenic acid have recently been shown to be essential and are included in this category as well.

B-Complex Vitamins

B vitamins perform a wide variety of functions. As a group (known as the *B complex*) they help the body metabolize protein, fats, and carbohydrates. They also help keep blood and the immune system strong. Good digestion, energy production, steady nerves, and healthy skin and eyes are all dependent on B-complex vitamins. Whole grains, nuts, seeds, dairy products, and organ meats (such as liver) are among the numerous sources of this vitamin complex.

Vitamin B$_1$, also known as *thiamine*, helps the body metabolize carbohydrates and proteins and is vital for a well-functioning nervous system. Thiamine also builds healthy blood, helps inhibit pain, and builds good muscle tone. Sources include whole grains, bewer's yeast, legumes, seeds, nuts, organ meats, and lean cuts of pork.

Dietary thiamine deficiency is prevalent in Southeast Asia, where the staple food is polished rice. This method of processing strips away the outer brown layer of bran, which contains thiamine. Active alcoholics, whose diets are frequently inadequate, often suffer from thiamine deficiency.

Extreme B₁ deficiency is called *beriberi* (an East Indian word for "weakness"). This ailment is common in developing nations. In *wet beriberi*, an individual's body retains water and swells with edema; heart failure often follows. Lack of thiamine in *dry beriberi* affects the nervous system and results in weakness of the arms and legs. Both of these variations are common in active alcoholics, who may suffer deficiencies of more than one vitamin. Another form of beriberi, *Wernicke-Korsakoff syndrome*, causes brain hemorrhage. Victims of Wernicke-Korsakoff are mentally confused and lose their memories and voices. In areas where polished rice is a staple food, many nursing infants between two and five months old die of infantile beriberi because of thiamine deficiencies in breast milk. Temporary *megadoses* of thiamine are used to treat beriberi. (Because vitamin megadoses can sometimes cause dangerous side effects, only a trained professional should prescribe them. Although there is no formal definition of a megadose, it is typically considered to be at least 10 times greater than the RDA.)

Vitamin B₂, also known as *riboflavin*, helps tissues use oxygen to produce needed energy. Riboflavin also contributes to healthy eyes and skin. Unlike other B-complex vitamins, this fluorescent greenish yellow substance is more plentiful in dairy products than in grains.

Individuals with an inadequate diet are at risk for riboflavin deficiency. Although this can affect the eyes, mouth, and tongue, such adverse effects are rare. Riboflavin is not toxic in large doses, but such doses do not seem to be particularly beneficial, either.

Vitamin B₃, or *niacin*, is needed to metabolize proteins and carbohydrates for energy production. It also plays a role in circulation, cellular growth, and the production of sex hormones and helps keep internal organs healthy. Whole grains, organ meats, fish, and nuts are some sources of niacin.

B₃ deficiency causes the condition known as *pellagra*. The disease is especially common in people with a diet based primarily on maize (a type of corn), because unless the maize is prepared correctly, the niacin in it cannot be used by the body. An individual with pellagra may experience sun-sensitive skin, weight loss, diarrhea, and mental disability.

Fruits are an important source of nutrients, including B-complex vitamins, vitamins A and C, iron, and potassium. Experts recommend five or more servings of fruits and vegetables daily.

Vitamin B5, or *pantothenic acid*, receives its name from the Greek word *pantos*, meaning "everywhere." B5 is an important component of acetyl coA, which, as discussed earlier, helps the body derive energy from food. A deficiency of this vitamin is rare, but active alcoholics—who are often B-complex deficient—are at risk. Upset stomach, susceptiblity to disease, and numbness in the hands and feet are common symptoms. Though B5 seems relatively safe in high doses, excess amounts provide no benefit. Meat, fish, eggs, dairy products, mushrooms, and oranges are sources of pantothenic acid.

Vitamin B6 is particularly essential for good nutrition. B6 plays a major role in the utilization of protein, which, in turn, keeps the body in good repair and helps maintain the immune system. B6 also helps the body use magnesium and linoleic acid. Women often find B6 beneficial in alleviating menstrual symptoms of bloating, tenderness, and tension.

Dietary deficiencies of B6 are rare, because the vitamin is found in many plant and animal foods. However, medication—including birth control pills and the tuberculosis drug *isoniazid*—will sometimes prevent proper metabolism of B6. Physicians often prescribe extra B6 to counteract this type of deficiency.

Large amounts of vitamin B_6 are present in foods with a high-fat content, such as nuts, avocados, wheat germ, oily fish, liver, and beef. Bananas and dried fruits such as prunes and raisins are also among the sources. The daily one or two milligrams of B6 that most people get from their diets is more than adequate.

Biotin is a B-complex vitamin found in organ meats and eggs. It is also produced by bacteria in the large intestine. Because only a few micrograms of biotin are needed daily, deficiencies do not occur in humans. Biotin is a coenzyme used in the manufacture of body fats and the synthesis of protein into glucose for energy.

Folacin, or folic acid, is another B-complex vitamin. It is essential for making DNA, the genetic material that is the basis of all living cells. As a result, an adequate supply of folacin is especially important when it comes to cells that must be produced rapidly and in large quantities, including immune, red blood, and bone marrow cells. In addition, folacin needs also increase whenever the rate of cell multiplication must be stepped up, such as after blood loss or injury, or during pregnancy.

Without adequate folacin, every system in the body suffers: The intestinal wall thins out and becomes unable to promote digestion and absorption; *anemia* (which results when the blood cannot carry adequate amounts of oxygen to the rest of the body) occurs as the number of red blood cells declines; and the immune system is weakened and more susceptible to disease. Mental confusion and lack of coordination also occur. Folacin deficiency is widespread throughout the world. Though many people show no obvious signs of deficiency, their bodies are not functioning at peak capacity. Women who take birth control pills require extra folacin, as do people who drink alcohol frequently.

Organ meats, orange fruits and vegetables, and wheat germ are all sources of folacin. These should be eaten raw or lightly cooked whenever possible because folacin is easily destroyed by heating.

Vitamin B_{12}, or *cyanocobalamin*, makes folacin available for certain metabolic reactions that help the body use iron, form blood, and maintain a healthy nervous system. Although found almost exclusively in animal products, it is also contained in certain yeasts and in *tempeh* (a fermented soybean product). A *vegan* (a vegetarian who avoids eggs

Food and Nutrition Board, National Academy of Sciences-National Research Council
Recommended Dietary Allowances (RDAs),[a] Revised 1989

Designed for the maintenance of good nutrition of practically all healthy people in the United States

Category	Age (years) or Condition	Weight[b] (kg)	Weight[b] (lb)	Height[b] (cm)	Height[b] (in)	Protein (g)	Fat-Soluble Vitamins Vita-min A (μg RE)[c]	Vita-min D (μg)	Vita-min E (mg α-TE)[d]	Vita-min K (μg)
Infants	0.0–0.5	6	13	60	24	13	375	7.5	3	5
	0.5–1.0	9	20	71	28	14	375	10	4	10
Children	1–3	13	29	90	35	16	400	10	6	15
	4–6	20	44	112	44	24	500	10	7	20
	7–10	28	62	132	52	28	700	10	7	30
Males	11–14	45	99	157	62	45	1,000	10	10	45
	15–18	66	145	176	69	59	1,000	10	10	65
	19–24	72	160	177	70	58	1,000	10	10	70
	25–50	79	174	176	70	63	1,000	5	10	80
	51 +	77	170	173	68	63	1,000	5	10	80
Females	11–14	46	101	157	62	46	800	10	8	45
	15–18	55	120	163	64	44	800	10	8	55
	19–24	58	128	164	65	46	800	10	8	60
	25–50	63	138	163	64	50	800	5	8	65
	51 +	65	143	160	63	50	800	5	8	65
Pregnant						60	800	10	10	65
Lactating	1st 6 months					65	1,300	10	12	65
	2nd 6 months					62	1,200	10	11	65

[a] The allowances, expressed as average daily intakes over time, are intended to provide for individual variations among most normal persons as they live in the United States under usual environmental stresses. Diets should be based on a variety of common foods in order to provide other nutrients for which human requirements have been less well defined.

[b] Weights and heights of Reference Adults are actual medians for the U.S. population of the designated age, as reported by NHANES II (the federal government's Second National Health and Nutrition Examination Survey). The median weights and heights of those under 19 years of age were taken from Hamill, P.V.V., Drizd, T.A., Johnson, C.L.,

and dairy products) should regularly include yeast and tempeh in his or her diet to avoid a deficiency of the vitamin.

B_{12} deficiencies often occur in individuals with stomach disorders (or who have had part of the stomach surgically removed), because the stomach secretes a substance that aids in the absorption of the vitamin. B_{12} injections bypass the absorption pattern and counteract this condition. Large doses of B_{12} are used only to treat deficiency and should

Recommended Dietary
Allowances
(RDAs),

Revised 1989

Water-Soluble Vitamins							Minerals				
Vita-min C (mg)	Thia-min (mg)	Ribo-flavin (mg)	Niacin (mg NE)[e]	Vita-min B$_6$ (mg)	Fo-late (μg)	Vitamin B$_{12}$ (μg)	Cal-cium (mg)	Phos-phorus (mg)	Mag-nesium (mg)	Iron (mg)	Zinc (mg)
30	0.3	0.4	5	0.3	25	0.3	400	300	40	6	5
35	0.4	0.5	6	0.6	35	0.5	600	500	60	10	5
40	0.7	0.8	9	1.0	50	0.7	800	800	80	10	10
45	0.9	1.1	12	1.1	75	1.0	800	800	120	10	10
45	1.0	1.2	13	1.4	100	1.4	800	800	170	10	10
50	1.3	1.5	17	1.7	150	2.0	1,200	1,200	270	12	15
60	1.5	1.8	20	2.0	200	2.0	1,200	1,200	400	12	15
60	1.5	1.7	19	2.0	200	2.0	1,200	1,200	350	10	15
60	1.5	1.7	19	2.0	200	2.0	800	800	350	10	15
60	1.2	1.4	15	2.0	200	2.0	800	800	350	10	15
50	1.1	1.3	15	1.4	150	2.0	1,200	1,200	280	15	12
60	1.1	1.3	15	1.5	180	2.0	1,200	1,200	300	15	12
60	1.1	1.3	15	1.6	180	2.0	1,200	1,200	280	15	12
60	1.1	1.3	15	1.6	180	2.0	800	800	280	15	12
60	1.0	1.2	13	1.6	180	2.0	800	800	280	10	12
70	1.5	1.6	17	2.2	400	2.2	1,200	1,200	300	30	15
95	1.6	1.8	20	2.1	280	2.6	1,200	1,200	355	15	19
90	1.6	1.7	20	2.1	260	2.6	1,200	1,200	340	15	16

Reed, R.B., Roche, A.F., and Moore, W.M.: Physical growth. National Center for Health Statistics Percentiles. Am J Clin Nutr 32:607, 1979. The use of these figures does not imply that the height-to-weight ratios are ideal.
[c] Retinol equivalents. 1 retinol equivalent = 1 μg retinol or 6 μg ß-carotene.
[d] α-Tocopherol equivalents. 1 mg d-α tocopherol = 1 α-TE (d-α tocopherol is one type of α tocopherol, that is, one type of vitamin E).
[e] 1 NE (niacin equivalent) is equal to 1 mg of niacin or 60 mg of dietary tryptophan.

otherwise be avoided. Although there is no clear evidence that they are toxic, megadoses of this vitamin have no known benefits.

Vitamin C

Vitamin C, or *ascorbic acid*, is vital for maintaining connective tissue. Healthy skin, bones, teeth, gums, blood, and blood vessels all depend on it. Vitamin C also promotes wound and bone healing, and iron absorption in the body depends on a steady source of ascorbic acid.

The story of vitamin C's discovery is well known. Seamen in the British navy commonly suffered from a disease called *scurvy*, which caused bleeding gums and loose teeth and slowed the healing process. In the 18th century, Dr. James Lind realized that something in lime juice prevented this disease from developing. Another 50 years passed before the navy decided to carry limes on their ships, but once this practice began, the incidence of scurvy decreased dramatically. (That is how British sailors became known as limeys.) Why limes solved the problem was unclear until 1932, when researchers working in two different labs were able to show that scurvy was caused by vitamin-C deficiency.

How much vitamin C humans need is still a controversial question. Most mammals can synthesize their own ascorbic acid, but bats, guinea pigs, higher apes, and humans all depend on external sources of vitamin C. Dr. Linus Pauling observed that primates in the wild consume much more vitamin C than the average human, leading him to propose that humans would benefit from greater amounts of this vitamin. In 1970, his book *Vitamin C and the Common Cold* recommended daily doses of up to 10,000 mg to prevent colds and reduce their severity. However, more than 20 experiments performed since then have not been able to show that extra vitamin C is effective in preventing colds. It has also not been proved that taking the vitamin can reduce the illness's severity. In addition, it has been found that populations in which great amounts of citrus fruit are eaten suffer less from certain cancers, but attempts to experimentally confirm the connection to vitamin C have been unsuccessful.

Some adverse effects from vitamin C megadoses have been reported. For example, any excess of the vitamin is excreted in the urine, making it more acidic, although it is unclear what effect this has on the body. Diarrhea and *urate stones* (solidified uric acid from the urine) may also occur. In addition, increased vitamin C dependency can result, since the body will become accustomed to higher and higher levels and need greater than normal amounts. However, if someone who has been taking megadoses for a long time cuts back, the body will eventually readjust.

Heavy drinkers may need somewhat more than the RDA, and smoking can cause certain metabolic changes that require larger doses of vitamin C as well. Citrus fruits, tomatoes, sweet peppers, berries, melons, broccoli, and potatoes are especially high in C. Vitamin C is sensitive to heat, light, and air, so that it is best to cook C-rich foods for only a short time, to avoid destroying a large part of the vitamin content.

FAT-SOLUBLE VITAMINS

A *fat-soluble vitamin* is one that dissolves only in fats and oils, which means that foods containing fats and oils also contain these vitamins. In addition, once foods containing vitamins A, D, E, and K are eaten, any excess is stored in body fat.

Vitamin A, or *retinol*, was the first vitamin to be identified and is found in such fatty-animal sources as cod liver oil. Carrots and other yellow vegetables, however, contain a substance called *beta carotene*, which is converted into vitamin A during the digestive process. Beta carotene is the major source of vitamin A in the diet.

The liver stores excess amounts of vitamin A and makes a protein that helps ferry the vitamin through the bloodstream and into the tissues. Vitamin A helps keep the retina of the eye functioning properly; it also plays a vital role in the health of bones, mucous membranes, and tissues inside the mouth, lungs, and other organs.

Vitamin A deficiency can result in roughened and peeling skin, and in more severe cases the condition can cause *night blindness*, an inability to see in low light or darkness. A lack of vitamin A can also prevent tissue from healing quickly. In children, deficiency may cloud the cornea—the clear membrane that protects the eye—and lead to permanently scarred eyes and blindness. This type of blindness is very common in developing countries. In addition, certain types of cancer seem to occur more often in populations with diets chronically low in vitamin A. Neither retinol nor beta carotene, however, have been found to have an effect on cancers already in progress.

Good sources of vitamin A or beta carotene include foods such as liver, fortified milk and dairy products, yellow and orange fruits and vegetables, and leafy green vegetables.

Too much vitamin A in the form of retinol is toxic and may lead to brain damage, headaches, nausea, vomiting, and blurred vision. Beta carotene does not seem to have any toxic effects apart from turning skin yellow.

Vitamin D helps the body absorb calcium and deposit it into the bones. It is found in fish oils, eggs, and fortified milk and dairy products. It is also produced in the body when the skin is exposed to the sun's ultraviolet rays.

Vitamin D deficiency in children is called *rickets*; in adults it is known as *osteomalacia*. Rickets was common in the United States and Europe through the early 20th century, when vitamin D was added to milk and other dairy products. Nonetheless, the disease is still a major problem in developing countries, where it cripples thousands of children. In *primary rickets* (rickets caused by dietary deficiency), bones become soft and bowed through lack of calcification or develop rows of small lumps. The bone deformity leads to pain and short stature. In osteomalacia, bones in the pelvis, spine, and legs lose minerals and soften. Legs bow, the vertebrae compress, and the pelvis flattens. Small doses of vitamin D can be used to treat both osteomalacia and primary rickets.

Secondary rickets (and osteomalacia) can occur when vitamin D is not properly utilized by the body. This can occur when the kidneys are damaged, because these organs are needed to "activate" the body's vitamin D supply. The problem is treated by giving the patient an already activated form of the vitamin.

Vitamin D is highly toxic in quantities only five times the RDA and leads to calcium deposits in tissues throughout the body.

Vitamin E, also known as *tocopherol*, receives its name from the Greek phrase "to bring forth offspring," because the absence of this vitamin causes sterility and stillbirth in lab animals. Vitamin E helps maintain cell membrane structure, and some people have speculated, although there is no solid scientific evidence, that megadoses of vitamin E can slow the aging process. Tocepherol may also help protect

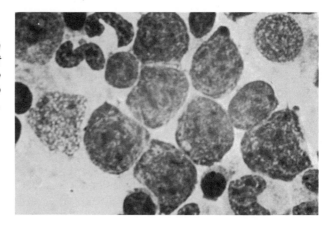

Iron deficiency can decrease the amount of hemoglobin in the blood, leading to anemia.

the body from being damaged by certain pollutants, and there is inconclusive evidence that it can offer protection against some cancers.

Vitamin E deficiency is rare, although premature infants may suffer from it because their bodies contain very little fat within which to store the vitamin. Deficiency leads to anemia because red blood cells become particularly fragile, but supplemental vitamin E is successful in reversing the syndrome.

It is not known whether prolonged megadoses of vita-min E are safe. Vegetable and fish oils as well as nuts are high in vitamin E.

Vitamin K was named for the Dutch word *koagulation*, because it helps synthesize the proteins that make blood coagulate, or clot. It is stored in the liver and released into the bloodstream as needed. Bacteria in the gastrointestinal tract are able to manufacture vitamin K as well. Deficiency is uncommon in adults. Infants, whose digestive tracts need time to develop friendly bacteria, are routinely given vitamin K by injection at birth. Normally, not even megadoses of K have been found to produce serious adverse effects. It is present in meats, milk and dairy products, cereals, fruits, eggs, and leafy green vegetables.

MINERALS

Minerals (or elements) differ from vitamins in that they are inorganic. Almost all of the 103 known elements on the periodic table are found in the human body, though not all of them are essential for its function.

The seven *macroelements*—calcium, phosphorus, magnesium, sodium, potassium, chloride, and sulfur—are present in relatively large quantities throughout the body and compose about 4% of total body weight. They help build bones, maintain body fluid at a near-neutral pH, maintain cell membrane structure, work with enzymes, and help transmit nerve impulses. With the exception of sulfur, the macroelements are also *electrolytes*, a type of salt. Electrolytes help maintain the proper level in body fluids by taking H+ ions away from solutions that are too acidic and releasing them into solutions that are too alkaline.

Trace elements, also known as *microelements*, are also present, but in minute quantities. These minerals include copper, fluoride, iodine, iron, manganese, zinc, chromium, molybdenum, cobalt, and selenium. They serve a number of functions, which include helping the body burn fuel and transport oxygen through the bloodstream in red blood cells. Trace elements are also used to form some of the components of proteins. Not all trace elements, however, serve a known purpose in the body.

Macroelements

Calcium is contained in the body in greater abundance than any other mineral. The average adult's body contains about three pounds of this mineral, almost all of it in the skeletal tissues. The remainder, about 1% or so, is present in body fluids and soft tissues. The body uses calcium to help secrete hormones, contract muscles, and transmit nerve signals. If the level of calcium in body fluids is too low for these functions to be carried out, calcium is taken from the bones to compensate. This leads to osteoporosis (see Chapter 7).

Though the RDA for adults ranges from 800 to 1,200 mg of calcium, some nutritionists recommend that women take between 1,200 and 1,500 mg. This is a concern in the United States because the generally sedentary American life-style contributes to bone loss, and the high levels of salt and protein in the typical American diet also leech calcium from the body.

Calcium is found in dairy products, sardines, nuts, and leafy green vegetables. Vitamin D and magnesium help the body absorb calcium. Absorption decreases, however, if these foods are eaten with those high in phosphorus (see **phosphorus**) and oxalic acid (which is contained in spinach, beet greens, and chard). Supplementary calcium is often taken in the form of calcium carbonate.

Sodium also has no established RDA, but the NRC's daily estimated minimum requirement for adults has been set at 500 mg. Amounts in excess of 3,300 mg, however, may cause high blood pressure in susceptible individuals. As a result, people with heart and kidney disease are generally put on low-sodium diets. Almost all processed foods contain added sodium, which is also found naturally in salt and dairy products, so deficiencies are rare. Athletes who perform in hot weather and perspire heavily might become depleted of sodium and feel nauseous and weak. A specially tailored sports drink can help replenish the supply.

Chloride is present in all body cells and is needed to maintain the body's delicate acid-base balance. Chloride is also present in acidic stomach secretions. No RDA has been established for chloride, but the estimated minimum daily requirement for adults is 750 mg. Deficiencies rarely occur, probably because the use of salt—a major source of chloride—is so widespread. It is not clear whether the chloride component of salt has any bearing on high blood pressure.

Potassium works with sodium to control the amount of water in body cells. Secretion of digestive juices, nerve-impulse transmissions, and both kidney and muscle function (including the heart's) all rely on potassium. There is no RDA for this mineral, but the estimated minimum daily requirement for adults has been set at 2,000 mg. Conditions that dehydrate the body, such as kidney disease, diarrhea, and the use of diuretics (substances that increase urination), may lead to potassium deficiency. In these situations, physicians will often prescribe a supplement. However, because excess potassium can cause irregular heartbeat, low blood pressure, and other problems, individuals should not take supplements without a doctor's approval. Bananas, dried fruits, peanuts, fish, yogurt, and most vegetables are foods high in potassium.

Sulfur is present in all proteins, and deficiency occurs only if an individual's diet contains absolutely no protein. Its most important job is its role in determining the shape of protein molecules.

Magnesium helps enzymes in the body store food and release energy. It is also important for maintaining muscle and nerve impulses, as well as calcium levels in the blood. However, megadoses of magnesium can have negative effects, producing drowsiness and dulling reflexes. Magnesium deficiency is rare in the United States, but anything that dehydrates the system will prevent the body from properly absorbing magnesium. Vegetables and cereals are among the sources of this mineral.

Phosphorus plays a role in the use of vitamins, fats, and carbohydrates for body energy; it also helps the body take in calcium for bones and teeth. Deficiencies are rare in the United States, but individuals who frequently use antacids containing aluminum hydroxide should be aware that these products can remove phosphorus from the body before it can be absorbed. Toxic effects from phosphorous are extremely rare, apparently because it is toxic only in large quantities and the body is able to effectively secrete the excess. Animal proteins, dairy products, eggs, legumes, and grains contain large amounts of phosphorous.

Microelements

Copper is needed to help absorb and metabolize iron. It is also a component of the enzymes involved in the use of oxygen during the Krebs cycle. The average adult body contains up to 150 mg of copper, stored in the brain, liver, kidneys, and heart. No RDA exists for copper, though an estimated safe and adequate intake ranging from 1.5 to 3 mg per day is recommended for adults. Because so many factors, including other nutrients, affect copper absorption and use, it is difficult to be sure how much is needed. Copper deficiency is rare in the United States.

There is evidence that more than 20 mg of copper per day might be toxic for humans, and if quantities are high enough, it may cause insomnia, high blood pressure, and mental illness. Shellfish such as lobster and oysters as well as nuts, organ meats, wheat, molasses, raisins, and olives are all sources of copper. Produce grown in copper-rich soil will contain somewhat higher levels of this mineral.

Fluoride is present in minute amounts in the body and improves the strength of teeth and bones. Much of the drinking water in the United States is *fluoridated* (meaning that fluoride has been added), but tea and fish also contain a good deal of fluoride. As little as one part fluoride to a million parts water is effective in reducing the incidence of tooth decay. There is no RDA for this mineral.

Iodine helps the thyroid gland produce a metabolism-regulating hormone. Sources of iodine include seafood, dairy products, and some plants. It is such an important nutritional element that most table salt in the United States is "iodized," which means that iodine has been added. However, certain foods eaten in large quantities—including raw cabbage, carrots, spinach, and brussels sprouts—interfere with the process by which iodine produces thyroid hormone. Iodine deficiency can lead to a condition known as *goiter*, in which the thyroid gland enlarges and the metabolism slows down, causing weight gain. Deficiency during pregnancy leads to physical and mental retardation in the unborn child. Deficiency during childhood can stunt a youngster's growth. Iodine overdose is rare.

Iron is a component of hemoglobin, which, as mentioned before, is the substance in red blood cells that carries oxygen from the lungs to the tissues. Iron is also found in the enzymes that metabolize energy from food. The amount of iron in the body is related to an individual's weight and gender. Men have 50 mg iron per kg (kilogram) body weight; women have 35 mg iron per kg body weight. (A kilogram equals 1,000 grams or about 2.2 pounds.)

The RDA for iron depends on an individual's age and sex. Because infants and children grow rapidly, they rely on a great deal of iron to form new body tissues and blood. Too little iron in the diet, pregnancy, problems with iron absorption, and bleeding may all lead to a deficiency. Because iron is needed to produce hemoglobin, a shortage of this mineral can cause anemia. Without an adequate supply of hemoglobin, the blood cannot carry all the oxygen the body needs. Anemic patients may become pale, weak, and tired.

Liver, dark meats, grains, dried fruits, leafy green vegetables, iron-fortified products, and molasses are iron sources. Cooking in a cast-iron skillet can also increase iron content because some of the metal will be absorbed by the food. Certain substances in eggs, green vegetables, and antacids interfere with iron absorption. The absorption of iron by the body is maximized by eating vitamin C–rich fruits and vegetables.

Manganese helps tendons and bones to grow. An RDA does not exist, but a daily intake of 2 to 5 mg is considered safe and adequate for adults. Coffee and tea, beans, nuts, and bran all contain manganese. Iron works against manganese absorption, but deficiency is rare. Although the toxic effects of manganese have not been found in people ingesting it through food, industrial workers exposed to excess manganese on the job have experienced adverse effects. These can include both neurological and behavioral disturbances.

Zinc is needed for physical growth and the metabolism of protein and carbohydrates. Zinc deficiency leads to ulcers, poor healing, a diminished sense of taste, and during pregnancy, zinc deficiency can retard the growth of the fetus. Slowed growth and impeded maturation are common in zinc-deficient children, especially if their diet is high in fiber, which decreases zinc absorption. Five hundred milligrams constitute a toxic dose of zinc and can cause nausea, diarrhea, and vomiting. Zinc impedes a copper and iron absorption. The RDA is easily obtained from animal products such as beef, organ meats, seafood, and cheese. Corn, whole wheat, nuts, seeds, and ginger are other sources.

Chromium helps body cells absorb glucose from the bloodstream. Without it, insulin cannot do its job, causing a condition that mimics diabetes. Chromium is sometimes used to treat adult diabetes; 50 to 200 micrograms per day is the estimated safe and adequate adult requirement. The toxicity of dietary chromium is extremely low, so that even large amounts do not appear to have adverse effects. Whole grains, cheese, molasses, liver, and brewer's yeast are sources of chromium.

Molybdenum helps metabolize substances called *xanthines*, which are found in coffee and tea as well as in animal proteins. No RDA exists, but a range of 75 to 250 micrograms per day is considered safe and adequate for adults. Molybdenum deficiency is rare. Industrial workers exposed to excessive amounts of this mineral can suffer from joint pain. Molybdenum is found in dark green vegetables, grains, nuts, legumes, and organ meats.

Cobalt is one of the components of vitamin B_{12}. Additional supplementation may be harmful, overstimulating the production of bone marrow and causing an enlarged thyroid gland or goiter. There is no RDA for this mineral.

Selenium contributes to healthy tissues and helps the pancreas function properly. Selenium also works with vitamin E to prevent harmful free radicals from forming during the breakdown of fat. In addition, a high selenium intake seems to lessen the risk of cancer, though it cannot cure the disease.

Multivitamin tablets are examined at a pharmaceutical manufacturing plant; vitamin supplements can be useful in some cases, but nutrients are best derived from food.

Deficiency is uncommon in areas where a variety of food from many different places is available. The amount of selenium in a given food depends on the selenium content of the soil from which it is grown. Selenium deficiency has recently been blamed for a disease long prevalent in a large area of China. Women of childbearing age and children were especially hard hit by heart-muscle degeneration and heart failure. A similar muscle disease was found in the area's cattle. By dusting crops with selenium and providing people with selenium supplements, the problem has been eliminated. Sources of selenium include whole grains, broccoli, fish and seafood, nuts, and garlic. Large doses of selenium over a long period of time may be toxic.

ARE VITAMIN SUPPLEMENTS NECESSARY?

A multivitamin supplement can be beneficial, but only when individuals are not getting a nutritionally balanced diet. These can include people on reducing diets, vegans, and individuals who smoke and drink. Pregnant women who are not getting an adequate diet may also be advised by their obstetrician to take a prenatal vitamin supplement. Again, it is important to avoid megadoses.

Multivitamins should be balanced, containing almost 100% of the RDAs for all vitamins and minerals except calcium, phosphorous, and magnesium. These three minerals should not be taken together—magnesium depletes calcium and phosphorus supplies, and phosphorus impedes calcium absorption. Even though no RDA for manganese exists at present, at least 5 mg of this element should also be present.

Unless one's diet is chronically deficient, it is not necessary to take vitamin supplements daily; one taken every two to three days is adequate. In addition, megadoses of vitamins are not generally recommended. As mentioned earlier, these tend to provide no benefits and sometimes prove toxic.

CHAPTER 7

NUTRITION THROUGHOUT THE LIFE SPAN

Dietary needs change throughout a person's lifetime. Periods of rapid development, such as during infancy, adolescence, and pregnancy, require additional calories and nutrients to build bone mass and new tissue. In addition, as people age, a healthy diet also helps to keep them vigorous and improves the quality of life. Moreover, certain diseases, including type II diabetes and high blood pressure, can often be controlled or reversed through diet.

HEALTHY HABITS

Many different institutions have published dietary recommendations. Among the most recent are those issued in 1989 by the National Research Council Committee on Diet and Health in their book *Diet and Health: Implications for Reducing Chronic Disease Risk.* The committee's recommendations are

- Reduce total fat intake to 30% or less of daily calories; saturated fats should comprise less than 10% of daily caloric intake; less than 300 mg of cholesterol should be consumed daily.

- Eat five or more servings of vegetables and fruits daily, with special emphasis on citrus fruits and green and yellow vegetables.

- Eat six or more servings of starches and complex carbohydrates (legumes, cereals, breads) daily.

- Eat only moderate amounts of protein.

- Use exercise and a balanced diet to maintain ideal body weight.

- Alcoholic beverages are not recommended, but individuals who drink should not consume more than two cans of beer or two small glasses of wine or two cocktails in a given day. Pregnant women should avoid alcohol altogether.

- Consume salty foods only occasionally; care should be taken to avoid oversalting food while cooking and at the table.

- Consume adequate amounts of calcium.

- If taking dietary supplements, do not consume more than the RDA.

- Fluoride intake is important, especially when baby and adult teeth are developing.

These guildelines are consistent with those issued over the past several years by the American Heart Association, the American Cancer Society, the American Dietetic Association, and many other organizations.

Milk is a good source of calcium, but experts recommend low-fat dairy foods.

The Milkmaid, Albert Cuyp (1620-91)

SPECIAL NUTRITION NEEDS FOR YOUNG AND OLD

Good nutrition is especially important for infants and children, because what they eat has a great impact not only on how they will develop and grow but also on the state of their health later in life.

Pregnancy

One of the best things a pregnant woman can do to ensure the health of her baby is to follow a sensible nutrition plan. A good diet increases the chances of having both an uncomplicated pregnancy and labor and of producing a robust and healthy infant. At least four servings of low-fat dairy products should be eaten daily as well as an additional serving of high-protein food. Women are advised to begin pregnancy at their ideal weight and to gain between 25 and 35 pounds. The extra weight will help their body accommodate various changes, such as the storage of fat in preparation for breast-feeding, as well as the growth of the placenta. This will also provide a reserve of nutrients for both the mother and her fetus. Underweight women should put on 35 pounds; those who are overweight may be advised to hold their additional weight gain to 20 to 25 pounds. Pregnant women need to raise their caloric intake by about 300 calories daily.

Pregnant women under 18 years of age need an extra nutritional boost. Besides being encouraged to gain 35 pounds during their pregnancies, younger women need 5 servings of low-fat dairy products as well as 4 servings of high-protein foods each day.

So as not to harm the developing fetus, avoiding drugs, alcohol, and cigarettes is strongly advised, and caffeine should be consumed in moderation, if at all. If a pregnant woman is a vegan, she may require a calcium supplement.

Infancy

Breast milk is the ideal food for infants and is the only food they need for the first six months of life. Along with supplying nutrients, mother's milk protects babies from certain allergies and diseases. The only mineral in which breast milk is deficient is fluorine, but the mother can take supplements to boost the supply. (Although most people live in areas with fluoridated water, infants do not drink enough water to benefit.)

Nutrition experts advise that five or more servings of fruits and vegetables be eaten daily, with a special emphasis on citrus fruits as well as on both green and yellow vegetables.

Breast-feeding women need 500 to 1,200 more calories daily than they took in before pregnancy. Furthermore, about 50 gm of protein should be eaten daily, and calcium, iron, and vitamins B and C are especially vital. If a balanced diet is carefully maintained, vitamin supplements may not be necessary. (Again, if the nursing woman is a vegan, calcium supplementation may be needed).

If a woman is unable to nurse, a commercially prepared formula is the next best thing to breast milk. Cow's milk should not be given to babies until the infant's physician advises it, because it contains more sodium and protein than the baby's system needs and is difficult for the infant to digest. Cow's milk is also too low in vitamin C, copper, and iron for a baby's nutritional needs.

By the time an infant is four to six months old, he or she can digest cereals and other starches and so may be slowly introduced to special infant cereals as well as strained vegetables and fruits. However, the baby should also remain on formula or breast milk for the remainder of the first year. Because the infant's system needs time to adjust to new foods, single-ingredient baby foods are best. These should be prepared without extra sugar or salt to avoid steering the child toward poor eating habits later in life. In addition, too much salt can put a strain on the baby's kidneys. Honey has been known to cause botulism in infants and should not be given to children less than a year old.

At first, only a few small spoonfuls of new foods are given to the youngster each day. From six to nine months, other new foods that may be introduced include fruit juices, strained meats, and plain toast or biscuits. Baby teeth begin to appear at about six months. From nine months to the end of the first year, chopped table foods can replace strained, single-ingredient foods. Soon the young child is eating miniature portions of most adult foods.

Children under age two should be given whole-milk dairy products and eggs. After that, a switch to skimmed-milk dairy products and a reduction in high-fat foods, such as eggs and animal products, should take place. However, fats and oils should never be completely eliminated from the diet.

Dieting

People embark on diets for a number of reasons. Many dieters have been warned by their doctors that excess weight is a complicating factor in conditions such as diabetes, cardiovascular disease, high cholesterol, and respiratory problems. Others want to lose weight in order to look and feel better, even if they are not actually overweight.

British psychotherapist Susie Orbach believes that many women have become overweight in response to Western culture's myriad and conflicting demands. Women have been made to feel that they must be attractive enough to find a mate, yet not so sexy that their appearance will cast doubt on their abilities in the workplace or on their mothering skills. Orbach's strategy for successful weight loss begins with teaching a woman to accept her body, even if she lacks the figure of a model or television actress.

Overall, however, there are a variety of contributing factors that can lead to weight gain, including the consumption of an excessive number of calories, insufficient exercise, or a predisposition among family members to become overweight (whether due to genetic or environmental factors).

According to the National Center for Health Statistics in Maryland, approximately one-quarter of adults in the United States are overweight. An individual is said to be *obese* if he or she is 20% or more above the average weight for his or her age, height, and sex. Obesity is the most prevalent nutritional disorder in the United States.

There are a number of ways to measure whether someone is overweight. Weight and height charts are derived either from population averages or from figures kept by life and health insurance companies listing weights that tend to be associated with the lowest death rates. A *caliper* can also be used to determine whether an individual is overweight. The instrument is used to pinch and measure the layer of fat beneath the skin.

There are both good and bad ways to shed excess pounds.

In this photo, circa 1900, it is not hard to see why this gentleman was declared winner of a "fat man's contest." However, obesity is a prevalent, and dangerous, medical disorder in the United States.

Among the harshest and most potentially dangerous methods are appetite suppressants; liquid or extremely low-calorie diets; surgery to remove fat, wiring the jaw together, or bypassing a portion of the intestine; fasting; eating strange amounts and combinations of food. These weight loss techniques may not only interfere with normal bodily functions but also can make it difficult to keep weight off in the long run. The best strategy is to adopt a permanent life-style change, including adequate exercise and a balanced, healthy diet. Extreme measures are advisable only for the very obese and only under close medical supervision.

Early Childhood

Parents often worry about how to feed their young children. Preschoolers are frequently disinterested in food and are picky eaters. However, young children often cannot eat a great deal in one sitting because their stomach is still small. A smaller breakfast, lunch, and dinner, accompanied by a midmorning and midafternoon snack, may be the solution. Parents can also become frustrated when a child refuses to touch certain foods but wants a favorite food every day. However, this is generally not a cause for concern. The youngster certainly will not starve and will eventually become interested in a wider variety of foods. In addition, children can be suspicious of mixed foods, such as tuna salad, and would rather see the individual ingredients and eat them separately.

Nonetheless, with a little creativity, a child can be encouraged to eat a varied diet. If, for example, a youngster hates vitamin A–rich squash, he or she may like cantaloupe, which is another good source of A. Letting children help shop for and prepare food can also make them more interested in eating it. Tasting new foods and sitting down to meals should be fun for children.

Fruit juice and low-fat milk are good substitutes for sugar- and caffeine-laden soft drinks in a child's diet.

The years between 6 and 12 are a time of slow, steady growth; good nutrition is a high priority. Healthy snacks of nuts, low-sugar cereals, fresh fruits and vegetables, and yogurt help supplement meals. Kids should be encouraged to go easy on caffeine- and sugar-laden soft drinks and opt instead for juices or low-fat milk. Because children learn eating habits by watching others, adults should try to set a good example.

Adolescence

The years between 13 and 16 are a time of rapid growth and development, so teens need to be especially nutrition conscious. Adolescents of both sexes will need more food and nutrients during puberty, although girls generally require 20% fewer calories than boys. This caloric restriction makes good nutrition somewhat more of a challenge for adolescent females. Girls also tend to be more body conscious and may emphasize slimness over healthy eating habits. Extremely low calorie diets or those that rule out entire categories of foods, such as carbohydrates, are unhealthy. Eating disorders such as *bulimia* (constant binging and purging) or *anorexia nervosa* (self-starvation) are especially dangerous and increasingly prevalent among teenage girls. (These disorders are described in greater detail in Chapter 8.)

Good nutrition for teens, however, does not mean ruling out fast foods and snacks altogether; it does mean making better choices. It can include opting for fresh fruits and vegetables rather than greasy, salty snack foods; having a slice of cheese pizza instead of french fries; eating low-fat dairy products; ordering unbuttered popcorn at the movies; adding some dried fruits and nuts instead of sugar to breakfast cereal; and drinking juices and herbal teas instead of soft drinks. Iron and calcium are especially important minerals for growing adolescents of both sexes.

Nutrition and Aging

Elderly people can also improve their health by eating properly. Taking in calcium-rich food helps keep bones and teeth strong, and drinking

Honey is a natural sweetener but does not contain enough nutrients to be considered any healthier than table sugar; it can cause botulism in infants.

six to eight glasses of water per day is especially vital for good digestion and kidney function at this stage of life. In addition, the fiber in fruits and vegetables helps prevent constipation and decreases blood cholesterol. Because illness or other factors may cause elderly people to eat less, smaller, more frequent meals can help some of them get the nutrition they need.

DIET AND EXERCISE

Athletes of all ages are often interested in how certain foods—especially protein—may improve their performance. The American Dietetic Association's position on nutrition for fitness is that very high protein diets do not result in a stronger body. In fact, the standard recommendation is that at least 55% of daily calories come from carbohydrates.

DIET AND DISEASE

High Blood Pressure

Individuals with *hypertension*, or high blood pressure, are put on moderate- to low-salt diets to lower their blood pressure. People with hypertension should also refrain from both using salt in cooking and adding it at the table and should avoid certain processed foods such as luncheon meats, salty junk foods, and pickles. In extreme cases, even unprocessed foods naturally high in sodium—such as dairy products—must be carefully regulated. Reaching one's ideal weight often helps control hypertension, too.

Cancer

According to dietary recommendations made by the National Cancer Institute in 1987, eating foods high in beta carotene (including apricots, sweet potatoes, carrots, and spinach) may reduce the risk of cancer. The same is true of vitamin C–rich foods, such as citrus fruits, strawberries, and broccoli. The institute also recommended raising fiber intake to 20 to 30 gm daily. Studies throughout the world have indicated that a low-fat diet is linked to a reduced risk of colon, rectal, breast, and uterine cancer. There also appears to be a relationship between eating large quantities of salty, brine-pickled, and smoked foods and the incidence of stomach cancer.

Osteoporosis

Osteoporosis is the condition of brittle bones most often found in post-menopausal women of Japanese, Chinese, and northern European descent. Loss of bone tissue and mass results in fragile, easily broken bones as well as a hunched back (also known as *dowager's hump*). Osteoporosis affects 500,000 women each year in the United States, often

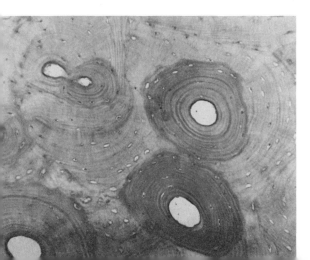

Bone cells in a patient suffering from osteoporosis; bones beome thin and fragile as the amount of tissue in them is reduced.

Health Foods

In their attempts at healthy eating, many people have turned to health food stores and cooperatives that sell less-processed foods and produce grown without pesticides. In order to better understand the benefits of these products, it is important to be familiar with certain terms associated with such foods.

Organic products are grown without chemical fertilizers, pesticides, or preservatives. Late in 1988, the Environmental Protection Agency (EPA), which controls the use of pesticides in the United States, reported that 66 pesticides used on food crops show limited evidence of being carcinogenic (cancer causing).

In general, organic foods are not only free from chemicals but also come from soil that has been chemical free for at least two or three years. Organic materials such as manure and bonemeal are used to fertilize crops, and certain natural methods, including "safe" plants and insects, are used to attack unwanted pests and weeds.

Organic foods are usually more expensive than those grown using more traditional methods because of the special attention they require.

However, not all states are consistent when it comes to labeling foods as organic. Some states have defined the term legally and certify the produce themselves. Others have defined the term but do not inspect the produce or hire an outside company to do so. Still, other states have set no standards for organic farming. The Organic Foods Production Association of North America (P.O. Box 1, Belchertown, MA 01007) has a list of organizations nationwide that have set their own standards for organic foods and that use them to certify products as such.

The words *natural* or *health food* are particularly difficult to define. Although some foods labeled with these terms may indeed be considered especially healthy, there are no regulations covering the use of these words and they may be employed simply as a marketing gimmick. To learn whether a food is truly nutritious, check the ingredients on the label.

Whole food is a term applied to unprocessed foods. For example, an apple is a whole food, but applesauce is not. Whole grains are those that have not been processed to remove the hull and bran, which are portions of the grain containing fiber and/or nutrients.

Organic foods are generally free from harmful chemicals. However, not all states have legally defined the term or certify foods as such, which means that one manufacturer's "organic" label may not mean the same as another's.

resulting in permanent, serious disability. Annually, about 40,000 to 50,000 women die of complications resulting from fractured and broken bones. According to *The Columbia Encyclopedia of Nutrition*, osteoporosis is the 12th most frequent cause of death in the United States. Women can do two things to prevent or retard the onset of the disease: One is to eat foods rich in calcium, especially during periods of rapid growth in adolescence and pregnancy. Another is to be physically active, since exercise stresses the bones, causing them to increase in mass and strength.

Diabetes

Diabetes is another common disorder related to diet. The pancreas manufactures and secretes insulin, which helps tissues absorb glucose, a source of fuel. In diabetes, either too little insulin is produced or the tissues are unable to respond to the insulin. Glucose then builds up in the bloodstream. Juvenile diabetes—which, as its name implies, occurs during childhood—is usually the result of a malfunctioning pancreas. Along with insulin injections, a carefully balanced diet is used to control the disorder. The form of diabetes that occurs in middle age, type II diabetes (also known as adult-onset diabetes), generally results from the tissue's poor response to insulin and can be controlled with the help of a well-balanced diet and by shedding excess pounds.

Diet and exercise are both essential to a healthy life-style, designed to keep the body fit and maintain ideal weight.

The diabetic diet is quite similar to the low-fat, high-carbohydrate plan currently recommended for general good health. It advises that

- 50% to 60% of one's daily calories come from complex carbohydrates.
- Refined sweets and junk foods be avoided.
- No more than 30% of the day's calories come from fats.
- 20% of the day's calories come from protein.
- Meals include plenty of fiber.
- Five to six small, frequent meals be eaten each day to help control the level of glucose in the bloodstream.

Following a diet that incorporates these rules encourages the pancreas to produce a slow, steady supply of insulin and as a result can help prevent *hypoglycemia*. This condition occurs when too much insulin is produced, causing tissues to absorb an abnormally high amount of glucose and leave too little in the bloodstream.

CAFFEINE

Caffeine is a stimulant found in coffee, tea, chocolate, aspirin and other over-the-counter medications, and in some soft drinks. Despite its wide availability, however, caffeine is considered to be a drug and can have different, and very noticeable, effects from one person to another. For example, the same two cups of coffee each morning that make one individual more alert and better able to function can leave another person irritated, anxious, shaky, and restless. Many people also develop a caffeine dependence and experience severe headaches after cutting down on caffeine or eliminating it from their diet for a day or two.

The amount of caffeine in a cup of coffee varies depending upon the way it was made. Drip coffee can have as much as 150 mg of caffeine in a 6-ounce cup, but the same amount of decaffeinated coffee contains only about 3 mg. Tea may contain anywhere from 25 to 60 mg of caffeine per 6-ounce cup, depending upon how long the leaves were steeped.

Coffee beans (left) being inspected by a farmer; tea leaves (right) being harvested in Tanzania; a 6-ounce cup of drip coffee can contain as much as 150 mg of caffeine.

Children get most of their caffeine from cola drinks and chocolate. Cola contains up to 50 mg per 12-ounce can or bottle, and a 6-ounce cup of cocoa or hot chocolate has about 10 mg. A 1-ounce chocolate bar contains about 6 mg of caffeine.

The effects of caffeine on the body are still unclear. Pregnant women are usually advised to lower their intake or eliminate it from their diet altogether. Animal tests suggest that high amounts of caffeine may stunt growth or lead to birth defects. In addition, there is some evidence that women who consume a great deal of caffeine during pregnancy are more likely to miscarry.

CHAPTER 8

GASTROINTESTINAL DISORDERS

Peptic ulcers result from an erosion of the lining of the stomach or duodenum. Symptoms can include searing stomach pain and vomiting.

Gastrointestinal disorders can make eating uncomfortable and affect how well food is absorbed and digested. Some disturbances of the digestive tract are caused by emotional responses to stress. A small child's excitement at a birthday party may lead to vomiting. A student facing an exam at school may suffer from an upset stomach and severe cramps. Many such gastrointestinal conditions, including *heartburn* and gas, are common and minor. Others, such as *ulcers* and diverticulosis, can produce more severe problems.

Physicians use a variety of techniques to diagnose gastrointestinal trouble. First the doctor will want to know more about the patient's symptoms—when and how frequently they occur, the type of pain or discomfort the patient experiences, how long it lasts, and under what conditions symptoms worsen or improve. X rays, *endoscopy* (use of an instrument with a lighted tip to view the inside of the body), and *computerized axial tomagraphy*, or CT scans (a series of X-ray "slices" that generate a cross-sectional image), are often used to provide the physician with a picture of the gastrointestinal tract.

COMMON MALADIES

Heartburn

Heartburn is the pain that results when acidic stomach contents are pushed up into the esophagus, a problem that often occurs when an individual bends over or lies down after eating. The stomach's contents sometimes regurgitate into the mouth (without nausea or the abdominal contractions of vomiting) and intense, burning pain is felt in the back, neck, back of the throat, or chest. As a result, a person with heartburn is sometimes convinced that he or she is actually experiencing a heart attack.

Normally the body works to prevent heartburn by using the *cardiac sphincter*, the muscular section at the base of the esophagus that keeps food from moving backward. However, fats, caffeine, mint, alcohol, and cigarette smoking relax the cardiac sphincter, allowing food to move in the wrong direction. People who suffer from heartburn should avoid irritating foods, try to wear clothing that fits loosely around the stomach, and refrain from bending over or reclining within the first three hours after eating. A doctor may recommend antacids to neutralize gastric juices or drugs to reduce gastric secretions.

Dyspepsia and Vomiting

Dyspepsia, or indigestion, is a feeling of fullness, discomfort, and pain in the upper abdomen or chest. Frequent burping, a distended belly, and

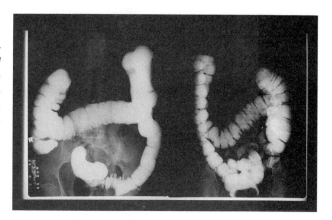

Diverticulosis (left) occurs when intestinal pressure forces the inner lining of the digestive tract to bulge through the outer muscular layer.

abdominal noises from excess gas and fluid are commonplace with indigestion. Nausea, lack of appetite, and a change in normal bowel habits also may occur.

Indigestion can sometimes indicate more serious problems, including a *peptic ulcer* and a gallbladder infection. Indigestion may also be caused by emotional stress or a rushed, heavy meal. Eating regular meals at a leisurely pace and in pleasant surroundings may help. Avoiding fatty foods, alcohol, caffeine, and spices for several meals is often beneficial as well. Occasional indigestion is generally nothing to worry about. If bouts become more frequent, a doctor should be consulted.

Vomiting occurs when the muscles of the abdomen contract involuntarily, the esophageal sphincter is open, and the stomach's contents are forcefully pushed up. Vomiting is one way in which the body rids itself of harmful substances—for example, after spoiled foods have been eaten.

Gastritis

Gastritis is an inflammation of the stomach's lining. An individual with gastritis may suffer stomach cramps, bloating, and loss of appetite or become nauseous and unable to keep food down. *Acute* (short-term) episodes can be brought on by stress, a reaction to aspirin, a food allergy, infection, food poisoning, or overindulgence in food and alcohol. Avoiding potentially irritating foods and beverages may help. If

95

the problem is severe enough to prevent a patient from eating solid food, he or she may have to substitute a liquid diet of water and nonacidic juices for a while, followed by a solid, bland diet.

In *chronic* (long-term) gastritis, the stomach's lining is damaged, rendering it unable to produce the usual supply of digestive juices. It is unclear what causes chronic gastritis, but a bland diet often helps to relieve discomfort. Because the damaged stomach lining has more difficulty absorbing vitamin B_{12}, patients should eat foods rich in this substance.

Constipation

Many people believe that a daily bowel movement is a sign of health, even if strong laxatives are needed to produce one. As long as there is no discomfort and pain when an individual does have a bowel movement, however, he or she is not constipated. When bowel movements are passed with difficulty, a range of dietary changes can remedy the problem. Eating more fiber-rich foods is one safe and effective treatment. Because fiber adds bulk to the stool, it speeds up the process of digestion and elimination. Twelve to 15 gm of fiber is the daily ideal, although most Americans get only one-third that amount. Drinking more liquids, especially prune juice, and increasing one's level of activity also help.

Diverticulosis

Lack of fiber is the main cause of another, more serious gastrointestinal problem called diverticulosis. In this condition, intestinal pressure forces the inner lining of the digestive tract to bulge through the outer muscular layer. The pouches that form sometimes fill with fecal material, resulting in infection and inflammation. Until this happens, a person with diverticulosis has no symptoms. When symptoms do occur, they may include alternating bouts of diarrhea and constipation, cramps in the lower abdomen, gas, bloating, and fever. If the pouches burst, the situation can be life threatening.

Severe cases are treated with hospitalization, bed rest, and intravenous fluids, as well as antibiotics to treat the infection. Damaged sections of the digestive tract are sometimes surgically removed. Milder cases can be treated by slowly adding more fiber to the patient's diet in the form of fruits, vegetables, and grains.

Sprue

Sprue occurs when diseases of the small intestine prevent normal food absorption. *Tropical sprue* often results when people accustomed to temperate climates spend extended periods of time in a tropical region. An infection of the small intestine leads to diarrhea, weight loss, anemia, and an inflamed tongue. Folic acid and antibiotics are used to treat the condition. *Nontropical sprue*, also known as *celiac disease*, will be discussed later in the chapter.

Diarrhea

Diarrhea refers to bowel movements that are unusually fluid and frequent. Food poisoning, infections, tension, certain drugs, spicy foods, or overeating may cause the intestines to either evacuate food too quickly for excess water to be absorbed or they may add extra water to the stool. Eating wisely and drinking plenty of liquids to replace lost fluid are usually helpful. If diarrhea persists for more than two days, a physician should be contacted.

Teaching rehydration techniques to parents in developing countries is an important step toward saving young lives. Millions of children die each year from diarrhea-associated dehydration and malnutrition.

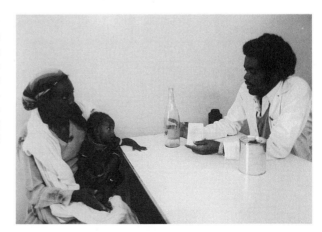

In terms of international health, diarrhea has the greatest negative impact on the nutritional status of children. Diarrhea often occurs when a water supply is contaminated and waste materials are improperly disposed of. The World Health Organization (WHO) estimates that in 1988, there were more than 1.36 billion cases of diarrhea worldwide (excluding China) in children under the age of 5. It has also been estimated that annually, more than 3 million children below age 5 die from diarrhea-associated dehydration and malnutrition. Giving a young patient mixtures of salt and sugar water or similar commercial preparations is vital in maintaining the child's health.

FOOD POISONING

Food poisoning is another source of gastrointestinal trouble and can be caused by bacteria, bacterial toxins or poisons, and, less frequently, by poisonous berries, fungi, and insecticides or other chemicals. Symptoms generally begin within 24 hours of eating contaminated foods and commonly include diarrhea, abdominal pain, fever, chills, nausea, and vomiting. Stools may contain blood and mucus.

Types of Food Poisoning

Salmonella bacteria are responsible for as many as 4 million cases of food poisoning in the United States annually. The microorganisms are found primarily in animal products, but they can also be contained in vegetables fertilized with manure or can be spread by unsanitary food handling. Symptoms appear within 24 hours of eating contaminated foods.

The infection is usually treated with bed rest. Individuals with salmonella are likely to experience severe diarrhea, so plenty of fluids and a bland diet are advised. Antibiotics are generally given to infants and the elderly because their systems are more vulnerable to the bacteria and easily dehydrated.

Staphylococcal bacteria thrive in cooked, warm foods, such as those available at cafeterias or salad bars. Symptoms occur up to eight

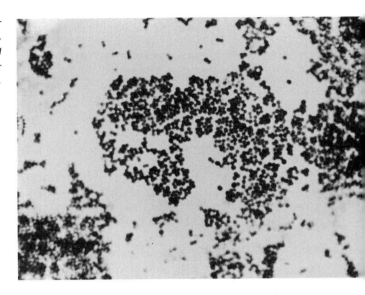

Staphylococcal bacteria live in cooked, warm foods, including those found in cafeterias and salad bars.

hours after eating contaminated food. Like salmonella poisoning, the infection is treated with bed rest. The condition should clear up by itself within about six hours.

Once vomiting slows or stops, the patient can have sweet, mild fluids such as soda or weak, sugary tea, or salty broth or bouillon. This may be followed by a bland diet. If an individual becomes severely dehydrated, he or she should be hospitalized and given intravenous treatment to restore fluid, sugar, and electrolytes.

Botulism is another form of food poisoning. It occurs infrequently and may incubate in the body anywhere from four hours to eight days after the toxin, a bacterium known as *Clostridium botulinus*, is ingested. Most people show symptoms 36 hours after eating contaminated foods, usually those that have been improperly canned at home. Nausea, vomiting, diarrhea, and abdominal pain are common and are followed by symptoms such as dry mouth, double vision, and decreased light reflex by the pupils. If untreated, the toxin can prove fatal by paralyzing muscles used in breathing. A physician can diagnose botulism by examining a patient's symptoms and analyzing food, blood, and feces. The condition is treated with medication that counteracts the bacteria.

ULCERS

An ulcer is an erosion of the lining of the stomach (*gastric ulcer*) or duodenum (*duodenal ulcer*). Both types are also referred to as peptic ulcers.

Duodenal ulcers are caused by acid and digestive enzymes secreted by the stomach. Physicians are still uncertain as to how gastric ulcers are formed, but the digestive enzyme bile may play a part. Cigarette smoking, poor nutrition, stress, and the use of certain drugs, such as aspirin, can also irritate or weaken the lining of the stomach or duodenum and sometimes play a role in the formation of ulcers. Too much caffeine may also be a factor, though this has not been proved.

Searing stomach pain is the first symptom of an ulcer, and vomiting may also occur. Whereas gastric ulcers usually cause pain after a meal, the discomfort of duodenal ulcers is sometimes relieved by eating. Bleeding follows if the damage continues to the level of the small blood vessels in the gastrointestinal walls. Too much blood loss can be fatal. *Peritonitis*, a severe infection, may set in if the lining itself becomes perforated, and this, too, may be fatal. In addition, scar tissue formed as the ulcer heals can cause obstructions. Surgery may be performed to repair or remove damaged areas. In a small number of cases, gastric ulcers can turn cancerous.

Antacids are often given to neutralize stomach acid, and prescription drugs such as *cimetidine* and *ranitidine hydrochloride* are frequently used to reduce acid production. It is important for people with ulcers to remain under a physician's care. Healing generally takes between four and eight weeks, although it is common for the condition to recur.

ILEITIS AND COLITIS

Ileitis is an inflammation of the ileum, the lower section of the small intestine. *Ulcerative colitis* occurs in the form of ulcers in the inner lining of the colon and rectum. Symptoms of both diseases include diarrhea, abdominal pain, fever, and rectal bleeding. It is estimated that, together, these disorders effect 2 million Americans, including about

200,000 under the age of 16. Although researchers still do not know the precise cause of ileitis and ulcerative colitis, evidence suggests that the body's own immune system may actually play a role.

Proper nutrition is an important part of treatment, particularly since these disorders can interfere with the body's ability to absorb nutrients, and because diarrhea and a reduced appetite also take their toll on a patient's health. Soft, bland foods may help make digestion more comfortable. Symptoms can also be treated with medication, but in severe cases, surgery may be necessary to remove damaged portions of the intestines.

FOOD ALLERGIES AND INTOLERANCES

When eating a given food triggers a reaction affecting breathing, the skin, or the nervous system, a *food allergy* may be the culprit. Symptoms include sneezing, congestion, rashes, nausea, and mental confusion. Nuts, seafood, corn, wheat, eggs, strawberries, milk, and chocolate are commonly involved in allergic food reactions.

Food intolerance also means that a given food causes a bad reaction. Unlike an allergy, however, a food intolerance does not involve the immune system. Symptoms of food intolerance include gas, diarrhea, nausea, and vomiting.

Two common examples of this condition are *lactose intolerance* and *gluten intolerance*. Lactose, as previously discussed, is a combination of the sugars glucose and galactose and is found in milk. Most babies are born with the lactase enzyme in their gastrointestinal tracts. The enzyme breaks the tie between the two sugars and allows them to be used by the body. In many people of Asian, Polynesian, and African background, however, lactase slowly loses its ability to work, so that by age 10 individuals with this condition find that it has become more difficult for them to digest milk. The problem does not affect the majority of North American caucasians.

Without lactase to break it up, lactose ferments in the digestive tract, producing irritating lactic acid. Within a few minutes of drinking milk, gases produced from the intolerant reaction cause stomach pain and distention. The intestine becomes irritated, and diarrhea may follow.

Intolerance to the protein gluten can result in painful reactions to foods made from gluten-containing grain, including wheat, rye, oats, and barley.

How much milk an individual with lactose intolerance can comfortably handle varies from person to person. Other milk products, such as cheese, yogurt, and buttermilk, contain less lactose and are therefore less likely to cause a problem. If necessary, milk substitutes made from soybeans and other foods can be used for drinking and in cooking.

Gluten intolerance is related to grain, not animal products. Gluten is a protein found in wheat, rye, oats, and barley. The condition, also known as celiac disease or nontropical sprue, becomes apparent within the first three years of a child's life. Symptoms of this disorder include constant, foul-smelling diarrhea, bloated stomach, poor appetite, and slow physical growth. Because even a tiny amount of gluten may set off painful symptoms, the youngster should avoid all foods containing the substance.

With time, some children may develop a tolerance to gluten, but others will remain sensitive to it throughout their lives. Every five years or so, a physician may slowly reintroduce small quantities of foods containing gluten. If successfully tolerated, the patient may make the transition to a normal diet.

Another ailment, *phenylketonuria* (PKU), is a rare genetic disease in which an infant's body is unable to convert the essential amino acid *phenylalanine* into another amino acid, *tyrosine*. Both amino acids are vital for normal growth, development, and body function. The buildup of excess phenylalanine can cause brain damage. A child with PKU is put on a low phenylalanine diet for life.

EATING DISORDERS

Sometimes physical illness seems to stem from cultural pressure and psychological problems. A predominant value in Western culture is that a slender body is the most desirable attribute that a woman can have. Many women have taken to heart the duchess of Windsor's saying: "A woman can never be too rich or too thin." Some have adopted this credo to such an extreme that they are endangering their health.

Anorexia and Bulimia

Bulimia and anorexia nervosa are two well-publicized eating disorders. According to the American Anorexia and Bulimia Association, approximately 1 million Americans are anorexic; 95% of them are white women in their teens and early twenties who come from middle- and upper-class households. Approximately 150,000 deaths directly attributable to anorexia occur each year. Anorexia is notably rare in times of war and in countries that often experience food shortages—it is most prevalent in the United States, Western Europe, and Japan. The disease's onset usually occurs in those less than 25 years old. In Greek, *anorexia* means "loss of appetite," and victims of the disorder routinely starve themselves to reach skeletal states. In bulimia—Greek for "ox eating"—an individual gorges herself with enormous quantities of food at one sitting; many sufferers immediately force themselves to vomit after a binge, or take diuretics and laxatives to keep off extra weight.

Although they are not new phenomena, the incidence of eating disorders has risen dramatically since the 1960s. Anorexia nervosa is classified as a psychiatric illness by the American Psychiatric Association in its *Diagnostic and Statistical Manual* (DSM-III-R). The DSM definition of anorexia includes

- Refusal to maintain a normal body weight.
- Weight loss of 15% (or more) below normal body weight.
- A distorted body image; feeling "fat" even though obviously emaciated.

- An intense fear of becoming fat and gaining weight.
- The absence of at least three consecutive menstrual cycles.

To help herself lose weight, an anorexic will often exercise to the point of exhaustion. As she becomes emaciated, a variety of physical and metabolic changes become apparent. A layer of fine hair called *lanugo* will cover her body, and her blood pressure, temperature, and pulse rate will decrease.

No one knows for certain why anorexia or bulimia occur. Some experts believe that anorexia is solely a physical disorder, like a cold or the flu. However, this theory cannot explain why anorexia is almost exclusively a woman's disease and why it occurs only in certain societies.

Psychologists have many ideas concerning the causes behind anorexia. Some see it as a young woman's attempt to control the physical changes of puberty. Others view it as a way of separating from one's family or, alternatively, as a way of crying out for more family nurturing. It is also suspected that anorexia may result from a faulty way of perceiving one's body. In addition, the denial of food resembles patterns seen in drug and alcohol abuse.

Therapeutic techniques include inpatient or outpatient psychotherapy and family counseling. If an individual is severely malnourished, tube feeding is used to bring her weight up to 80% of the ideal. Gaining weight beyond that point is the patient's responsibility as she tries to reestablish normal eating habits. After a long period of time away from food, most anorexics have difficulty eating even if they want to. Whether or not treatment succeeds varies from one patient to another. More than half of all anorexics under care are unable to resume normal eating patterns, and relapses are common. Six percent of those hospitalized for anorexia die from a lack of nutrients in the blood due to starvation (as did popular singer Karen Carpenter in 1983) or electrolyte imbalance. One percent of those hospitalized commit suicide.

Nutritious low-calorie meals can put Americans on the road to a longer, healthier life.

Eating disorders can also be treated through Overeaters Anonymous, a group that provides a plan to deal with food that is similar to the one used by Alcoholics Anonymous to handle alcohol abuse.

Six percent of American women are bulimic. Occasional bulimic behavior is common in up to 25% of college-age women, and the problem often begins when an individual decides to diet. Features of bulimia include

- Episodes of binge eating that, according to the DSM, occur at least twice a week for three months. (However, because bulimia appears to be a progressive illness, not all eating disorder specialists agree that binges must be so frequent.)

- Feeling lack of control during eating binges.

- Self-induced vomiting, laxative or diuretic abuse, excessive exercise, or excessively strict dieting to control weight gain.

- Obsession with weight and body shape.

Some anorexics also binge and purge. The constant vomiting irritates the salivary glands, wears away the tooth enamel, abrades the esophagus, and may cause *hiatal hernia*, in which part or all of the stomach pushes into the chest cavity through the hole leading to the esophagus. Bulimics often become dehydrated. If the body's normal electrolyte balance is disrupted, disturbances of the heart rhythm may follow, ultimately ending in premature death. Behavioral therapy may help bulimic individuals gain more control over their eating habits.

Another disorder, known as *pica*, is a condition in which an individual eats nonnutritional or harmful substances such as grass, dirt, stones, paint chips, or cloth. Pica is observed in young children, mentally handicapped or disturbed individuals, and sometimes in pregnant women. Folk wisdom has it that pica occurs because of vitamin or mineral deficiencies, such as a shortage of iron in the body. It is classified as a psychiatric disorder in the American Psychiatric Association's DSM.

CONCLUSION

Clearly, nutrition is a complex subject that goes far beyond simply filling an empty stomach. There are many choices to make concerning the types of food to be eaten, alternatives that hinge on factors ranging from an individual's age and health to his or her life-style and emotional state. Through moderation and careful planning, however, a well-informed consumer can make the kinds of selections that lead to a longer, healthier life.

APPENDIX:
FOR MORE INFORMATION

The following is a list of associations and organizations that can provide more information on nutrition, eating disorders, digestive diseases and disorders, and related subjects.

GENERAL INFORMATION

American Cancer Society
1599 Clifton Road NE
Atlanta, GA 30329
(404) 320-3333

The American Dietetic Association
216 West Jackson Blvd.
Chicago, IL 60606-6995
(312) 899-0040

American Heart Association
7320 Greenville Avenue
Dallas, TX 75231
(214) 373-6300

Center for Science in the Public Interest
1875 Connecticut Avenue NW
Washington, DC 20002
(202) 373-6300

Egg Nutrition Center
2301 M Street NW, Suite 405
Washington, DC 20037
(202) 883-8850

Food and Drug Administration
Office of Consumer Affairs

5600 Fishers Lane, HFE-88
Rockville, MD 20857
(301) 443-3170

National Institute of Nutrition
1565 Carling Avenue, Suite 400
Ottawa, Ontario K1Z 8R1
Canada
(613) 725-1889

Office of Disease Prevention and Health
    Promotion
National Health Information Center
P.O. Box 1133
Washington, DC 20013-1133
(800) 565-4167
(in Maryland)
(800) 336-4797
(outside Maryland)

U.S. Department of Agriculture
Food Safety and Inspection Service
Washington, DC 20250
Meat and Poultry Hotline:
(800) 447-3333
(in Washington, DC)
(800) 535-4555
(outside Washington, DC)

DIGESTIVE DISEASES

American Liver Foundation
1425 Pompton Avenue
Cedar Grove, NJ 07009
(201) 857-2626
(800) 223-0179

Canadian Foundation for Ileitis and
    Colitis
21 St. Clair Avenue East, Suite 301
Toronto, Ontario M4T 1L9
Canada
(416) 920-5035

Crohn's Colitis Foundation of America
444 Park Avenue South
New York, NY 10016
(212) 685-3440

National Digestive Disease Education
    and Information Clearinghouse
Box NDDIC
Bethesda, MD 20892
(301) 468-6344

EATING DISORDERS

American Anorexia and Bulimia
    Association
418 East 76th Street
New York, NY 10021
(212) 734-1114

Anorexia and Bulimia Resource Center
255 Alhambra Circle, Suite 32
Coral Gables, FL 33134
(305) 444-3731

Anorexia Nervosa and Related Eating
    Disorders, Inc.
P.O. Box 5102
Eugene, OR 97405
(503) 344-1144

Bulimia Anorexia Self-Help
P.O. Box 39903

St. Louis, MO 63139
(800) 227-4785
Crisis Line: (800) 762-3334

Center for the Study of Anorexia and
    Bulimia
1 West 91st Street
New York, NY 10024
(212) 595-3449

Food and Nutrition Information Center
National Agricultural Library
10301 Baltimore Blvd., Room 304
Beltsville, MD 20705
(301) 344-3719

National Eating Disorder Information
    Center
200 Elizabeth Street
College Wing I-328
Toronto, Ontario M5G 2C5
Canada
(416) 340-4156

Overeaters Anonymous
World Service Office
4025 Spencer Street, #203
Torrance, CA 90503
Mail address: P.O. Box 92870
Los Angeles, CA 90009
(213) 542-8886

OSTEOPOROSIS

National Osteoporosis Foundation
2100 M Street NW, Suite 602
Washington, DC 20037
(202) 223-2226

Osteoporosis Society of Canada
76 St. Clair Avenue West
Suite 502
Toronto, Ontario M4V 1N2
Canada
(416) 922-1358

FURTHER READING

GENERAL INFORMATION

Bennett, William, and Joel Gurin. *The Dieter's Dilemma.* New York: Basic
 Books, 1983.

Bolt, Robert J., et al. *Digestive System.* New York: Wiley, 1983.

Bosco, Dominick. *The People's Guide to Vitamins and Minerals: From A to
 Zinc.* Chicago: Contemporary Books, 1980.

Brooks, Svevo. *Common Sense Diet and Health.* Santa Cruz: Botanica, 1987.

Carlson, Linda. *Food and Fitness.* Los Angeles: Price Stern, 1988.

Consumer Guide Editors. *Rating the Diets.* New York: New American
 Library, 1986.

Gossel, Thomas A., and Donald W. Stansloski. *The Complete Medicine Book.*
 New York: Crescent Books, 1987.

Hausman, Patricia. *Foods That Fight Cancer.* New York: Warner, 1985.

Natow, Annette B., and Jo-Ann Heslin. *No-Nonsense Nutrition for Kids.* New
 York: Pocket Books, 1986.

———. *Nutrition for the Prime of Your Life.* New York: McGraw-Hill, 1984.

Pauling, Linus. *Vitamin C, the Common Cold, and the Flu.* San Francisco: Freeman, 1976.

Smith, Lendon. *Feed Yourself Right.* New York: Dell, 1984.

Wade, Carlson. *Fact Book on Fats, Oils, and Cholesterol.* New Canaan, CT: Keats, 1973.

DIGESTIVE DISEASES AND DISORDERS

Goldberg, Myron D., and Julie Rubin. *The Inside Tract: The Complete Guide to Digestive Disorders.* New York: Beufort, 1982.

Lay, Joan. *Diets to Help Colitis.* New York: Sterling, 1988.

Mendeloff, Albert, and James P. Dunn. *Digestive Diseases.* Cambridge: Harvard University Press, 1971.

Sorenson, Joyce, and Nancy Murray. *Digestive Disorders.* Hartford, CT: Witkower Press, 1983.

EATING DISORDERS

Brumberg, Joan Jacobs. *Fasting Girls: The Emergence of Anorexia Nervosa as a Modern Disease.* Cambridge: Harvard University Press, 1988.

Erlanger, Ellen. *Eating Disorders: A Question and Answer Book About Anorexia Nervosa and Bulimia Nervosa.* Minneapolis: Lerner, 1987.

Hirschmann, Jane, and Carol Munter. *Overcoming Overeating: Living Free in a World of Food.* Indianapolis: Addison-Wesley, 1988.

Palmer, R. L. *Anorexia Nervosa: A Guide for Sufferers and Their Families.* London: Penguin, 1981.

GLOSSARY

acetyl coenzyme A acetyl coA; a chemical that, along with oxaloacetic acid, initiates the Krebs cycle

acid a sour water-soluble compound that has a positive charge and a pH of less than 7

acute characterized by sudden onset and short duration

alimentary canal digestive system; the digestive tube extending from the mouth to the anus

alkaline base; a water-soluble compound with a negative charge and a pH of more than 7

amino acid the building block of proteins

anemia a condition resulting from too little hemoglobin in the blood; can be caused by a deficiency of iron; characterized by weakness, pallid complexion, and exhaustion

anorexia nervosa an eating disorder characterized by a distorted self-image and by self-starvation

antacid an agent, such as an alkaline, that neutralizes acidity

basal metabolism the amount of energy needed to maintain vital body functions when the body is at rest and the stomach is empty

bile an alkaline substance manufactured by the liver that emulsifies fats so that they may be digested

binge the activity, practiced by bulimics, of eating large amounts of food

botulism a potentially fatal food poisoning caused by a toxic substance produced by bacteria in food; characterized by nausea, vomiting, diarrhea, abdominal pain, dry mouth, and double vision

bulimia an eating disorder characterized by a constant craving for food, binge eating, induced vomiting, and the taking of diuretics or laxatives

cancer any malignant tumor that destroys normal tissue as it spreads to adjacent tissue layers or to other parts of the body

carbohydrates a group of organic compounds of carbon, hydrogen, and oxygen; generally produced by plants; one of the three main constituents of food; the body's primary source of energy

cardiac sphincter a thick muscular ring around the opening between the esophagus and stomach; keeps food from moving backward

cellulose an indigestible carbohydrate found in the cell walls of plants; a form of dietary fiber

chyme the thick liquid that is formed as the stomach kneads eaten food

cholesterol a fatty substance produced by the body and found in foods derived from animal products; proven to increase risk of cardiovascular disease

chronic characterized by long duration or frequent recurrence

diabetes mellitus a disease characterized by an excess of undigested sugar in the blood, due to an inadequate secretion or utilization of insulin

diarrhea abnormally frequent bowel movements marked by fluid stools

dietitian a specialist in the science of applying the principles of nutrition to diet

digestion the process by which food is prepared for its use in the body

disaccharides sugars composed of two monosaccharide sugar molecules; along with monosaccharides, are called simple sugars

diverticulosis an intestinal disorder caused by the formation of pouches of fecal matter in the digestive tract; characterized by diarrhea, constipation, cramps, gas, bloating, and fever

enzyme a protein that is produced by a living cell and triggers certain chemical reactions

essential amino acids the nine amino acids that the human body must obtain from food

essential fatty acids fatty acids not produced by the human body; obtained from food

fats compounds of carbon, hydrogen, and oxygen made from glycerol and fatty acid; one of the three principal constituents of food; the main substance into which excess carbohydrates are converted for storage by the human body

fat-soluble vitamins vitamins capable of dissolving only in fats and oils

fiber roughage; food that is high in indigestible plant material

fructose a simple sugar, or monosaccharide, found in fruit

free radicals unstable molecules created during the Krebs cycle that roam through the body oxidizing and destroying tissues and cells; believed to hasten aging and cause cancer

galactose a simple sugar, or monosaccharide, that is part of the sugar in milk

gallbladder a membranous, muscular sac that stores bile and squeezes it into the duodenum during the digestive process

gastric juice acidic fluid containing hydrochloric acid and secreted by cells lining the stomach; aids in the digestion of proteins and fats

gastrointestinal tract the stomach and intestines

glucose a simple sugar, or monosaccharide; the main constituent of table sugar

hypertension abnormally high blood pressure

hypoglycemia abnormally low blood sugar caused by the production of too much insulin

ileitis an inflammation of the lower section of the small intestine; characterized by diarrhea, abdominal pain, fever, and rectal bleeding

inorganic composed of matter that does not contain carbon

insulin a hormone produced by the pancreas that helps cells take in glucose

kidneys two bean-shaped organs located toward the back at waist level that remove waste and excess water from the blood as urine

Krebs cycle citric acid cycle; a series of chemical reactions that take place in every living organism by which glucose is broken down and energy is produced

kwashiorkor a condition in which there is a deficiency of protein but not of other nutrients; characterized by stunted growth and the impairment of the body's ability to repair itself

lactase a digestive enzyme that breaks down the sugar lactose

lactose milk sugar; a disaccharide made from galactose and glucose

large intestine the final portion of the alimentary canal; stores undigested food and removes wastes through the rectum and the anus

lipase a digestive enzyme that helps break down fats into fatty acids

lipoproteins a fat and protein unit that is carried through the bloodstream and used by the body

liver a large organ located in the upper-right abdomen; converts sugar to glycogen and also secretes bile

maltase a digestive enzyme that breaks down the sugar maltose

maltose barley sugar; a disaccharide composed of two glucose molecules

marasmus a condition resulting from undernourishment or disease, occurring especially in children; often caused by a protein-deficient diet

metabolism the process through which the body makes chemical changes in nutrients to create energy and new materials

minerals inorganic substances, some of which are necessary to nutrition

monosaccharides sugars that are not reducible to simpler sugars; along with disaccharides, are referred to as simple sugars

mucin a lubricating fluid found in saliva that makes food easier to swallow

nutrients substances vital for energy, growth, development, and repair of an organism

nutrition the process by which an animal or plant consumes and utilizes food; also, the science that examines this process

omnivorous consuming both plant and animal products

organic containing carbon compounds

osteoporosis a disease characterized by loss of bone tissue; caused by nutritional deficiency

oxaloacetic acid a chemical that, along with acetyl coenzyme A, initiates the Krebs cycle

pancreas a tongue-shaped organ located at the back of the abdomen; secretes a variety of digestive enzymes as well as insulin, a hormone essential for the metabolism of carbohydrates

pectin a form of dietary fiber

pellagra a condition caused by vitamin B_3 deficiency; characterized by sun-sensitive skin, diarrhea, weight loss, and mental disability

pepsin an enzyme that works with gastric juices to break down proteins into amino acids

peptic ulcer an ulcer on the wall of the stomach or on the duodenum resulting from erosion of the lining

peristalsis an involuntary wavelike muscle movement passing along the walls of certain hollow muscular structures in order to propel contents onward

peritonitis a severe infection of the lining of the stomach

pH scale a scale to measure the concentration of hydrogen-ion activity in a solution; used to ascertain whether a solution is alkaline or acidic

polypeptidase a digestive enzyme that breaks down proteins into their constituent amino acids

polysaccharides complex carbohydrates; chains of glucose molecules linked together in straight lines or in a branching structure

proteins complex molecules consisting of a combination of amino acids; one of the three main constituents of food; an essential part of all living cells

ptyalin a digestive enzyme found in saliva

rickets a disease in children sometimes caused by vitamin D deficiency; characterized by soft and deformed bones; called osteomalacia in adults

saliva a digestive juice secreted into the mouth

salmonella bacteria found primarily in animal products

scurvy a disease caused by vitamin C deficiency; characterized by bleeding gums, loose teeth, and the slow healing of wounds

spleen a small, ductless gland that lies just above the left kidney; destroys old blood cells, stores blood, produces white blood cells, and acts as a storage organ for iron and copper

staphylococcus bacteria that thrive in cooked, warm foods; a common cause of food poisoning

starch a polysaccharide found in plant foods such as potatoes, grains, and beans

sucrase a digestive enzyme that breaks down the sugar sucrose

sucrose cane and beet sugar; the disaccharide combination of glucose and fructose

vegan a strict vegetarian; one who eats no animal or dairy products

villi fingerlike projections lining the small intestine that absorb nutrients and pass them into the bloodstream

vitamins any of various organic substances that in small amounts are essential to the regulation of metabolic function

water-soluble vitamins vitamins capable of dissolving only in water; not easily stored in the body

INDEX

PICTURE CREDITS

Anne Galperin, a freelance writer on health issues, computers, and other subjects, is a graduate of Northwestern University. She has worked as a writer for *Windy City Times*, a national gay and lesbian newsweekly, and has tutored teenagers at Old Orchard Psychiatric Hospital in Skokie, Illinois.

Dale C. Garell, M.D., is medical director of California Children Services, Department of Health Services, County of Los Angeles. He is also associate dean for curriculum at the University of Southern California School of Medicine and clinical professor in the Department of Pediatrics & Family Medicine at the University of Southern California School of Medicine. From 1963 to 1974, he was medical director of the Division of Adolescent Medicine at Children's Hospital in Los Angeles. Dr. Garell has served as president of the Society for Adolescent Medicine, chairman of the youth committee of the American Academy of Pediatrics, and as a forum member of the White House Conference on Children (1970) and White House Conference on Youth (1971). He has also been a member of the editorial board of the *American Journal of Diseases of Children.*

C. Everett Koop, M.D., Sc.D., is former Surgeon General, deputy assistant secretary for health, and director of the Office of International Health of the U.S. Public Health Service. A pediatric surgeon with an international reputation, he was previously surgeon-in-chief of Children's Hospital of Philadelphia and professor of pediatric surgery and pediatrics at the University of Pennsylvania. Dr. Koop is the author of more than 175 articles and books on the practice of medicine. He has served as surgery editor of the *Journal of Clinical Pediatrics* and editor-in-chief of the *Journal of Pediatric Surgery*. Dr. Koop has received nine honorary degrees and numerous other awards, including the Denis Brown Gold Medal of the British Association of Paediatric Surgeons, the William E. Ladd Gold Medal of the American Academy of Pediatrics, and the Copernicus Medal of the Surgical Society of Poland. He is a chevalier of the French Legion of Honor and a member of the Royal College of Surgeons, London.